D1432804

THE MAN WHO WAS PRIVATE WIDDLE

by the same author

REWARDS AND FAIRIES by Rudyard Kipling
An Edition
STAGE PEOPLE
A Harlequinade
THE MEMOIRS AND CONFESSIONS OF A JUSTIFIED SINNER
by James Hogg
An Introduction
THE LIFE AND DEATH OF PETER SELLERS
An Elegy
THE REAL LIFE OF LAURENCE OLIVIER
A Romance

forthcoming

INSIDE ANTHONY BURGESS
An Anatomy
KILL FEES
A Gathering
NEVER TRUST A BEARDED MAN
A Journal
THE LIFE AND OPINIONS OF ANDREW AGUECHEEK
A Novel
BACK TO THE SLAUGHTERHOUSE
An Autobiography
THE CHINESE ARE IN TORQUAY
A Mystery

The Man who was Private Widdle
CHARLES HAWTREY
1914–1988

Roger Lewis

faber and faber

First published in 2001
by Faber and Faber Limited
3 Queen Square London WC1N 3AU

Typeset by Refinecatch Limited, Bungay, Suffolk
Printed in England by Clays Ltd, St Ives plc

A CIP record for this book is available from the British Library

ISBN 0–571–21064–3

2 4 6 8 10 9 7 5 3 1

'The only Englishmen, living in England, who remain wholly eccentric beyond middle-age are those who go mad.'

Kenneth Tynan, *Persona Grata*

CONTENTS

Acknowledgements, ix

Part One: Art, 1

Entr'acte, 45

Part Two: Life, 59

Epilogue, 95

Appendix, 99

Select Bibliography, 109

Index, 111

ACKNOWLEDGEMENTS

He was like a man, as Falstaff said of Justice Shallow, 'made after supper of a cheese-paring'; and though, in the past, I have written about big stars, big personalities, Charles Hawtrey, this will-o'-the-wisp from the *Carry On* series, whilst he was never going to knock Laurence Olivier or Peter Sellers off their high shelf, nevertheless had a distinctive character (there's no mistaking who he was) that appeals to my taste for the misunderstood, the disconsolate and the bizarre. He seems to me a performing-arts equivalent of a minor nineteenth-century poet or short-story writer; Calverley, say, or A. E. Coppard, who exist in treasurably slim, slightly foxed dusty first editions.

In his time, Hawtrey was much loved by the public, yet he ended his days on the Kent coast an ungracious mad drunkard.* Sallow-faced and as slender as a hazel twig, he may

---

* What, when there are places on the map called Upper Dicker, Lower Dicker, or Wyre Piddle, was the particular appeal of Deal (pop. 28,504), one wonders, for the nation's reprobates and misanthropes? The drunken polymorphously perverse bankrupt novelist and cashiered King's Own Shropshire Light Infantryman Simon Raven (1927–2001), for example, was banished to a nursing home for handicapped old ladies in the town for thirty-four years, sallying forth every now and again to a massage parlour opposite the Reform Club, Pall Mall, for 'a good housemaid's wank'. One is compelled to picture the streets of Deal as a world in decay thronged with George Grosz characters got up in askew velvet hats and musquash coats seeking eyeglass-fogging diversions. 'I always used to see Hawtrey being pulled out of pubs,' Raven recalled the week before he died. 'But what's wrong with that? We all like a drink, don't we dear?' Deal is the capital of non-conformity.

still make us laugh as Private Widdle, of the Queen's Own Third Foot and Mouth Regiment ('the Devils in Skirts'), patrolling the North West Frontier in his calf-length kilt ('It fairly whistles up the Pass'); but how funny was it when he was rebuffed and humiliated night after night in his fruitless, pie-eyed attempts to seduce a recruit from the Royal Marines School of Music or when he loitered on the links hoping to catch the eye of the Caddie Master of the Royal Cinque Ports Golf Club? (Well – it's still funny, but it's also sordid and sad.)

'For all the world he was like a forked radish' (Falstaff on Shallow again – a role Hawtrey should have played), 'with a head fantastically carved upon it with a knife; he was so forlorn ... yet lecherous as a monkey.' Having spent these past few months examining his career, I think there was an adagio aspect to his acting, an air of being unfulfilled, which accounts for an off-stage, off-screen existence that was full of dark moments; and the first people I must thank in my quest to understand Hawtrey better are the townspeople of Deal and Walmer, who had to endure his antics for about sixteen years: Bill Bennett (formerly of Pickards the Butchers in Upper Walmer, latterly a disc jockey for the Gateway Hospital Broadcasting Service, Buckland Hospital, Dover); Lizzie Cook (*East Kent Mercury*); Wayne Cox (Abbey Direct Home Sales); Nick Henwood (Strategic Director, Deal Library); and the staff at the Tourist Information Office and Deal Town Hall.

Morris Bright, who, with his writing partner Robert Ross, is the encyclopaedic *Carry On* historian, was generous with his time; Colin Bourner kindly handed over his research material for a (now abandoned) book on the *Carry On*s; Patrick Newley provided a list of eye-witnesses; Mo Rowbotham and Jez Dolan (Arts Development Officer, Stockport

Acknowledgements

Arts Team) gave me news about Hawtrey at the Romiley Forum; and Carl St. John, of the Kenneth Williams and Sidney James Society, sent me useful clippings.

The Matron of Denville Hall, the editor of *The Stage*, and the literary editors of the *Mail on Sunday* (Susanna Gross) and *The Spectator* (Mark Amory) helped to spread news of my project abroad; and I'm grateful to those who responded to my appeals for information, especially Richard Hatton, Kevin Jewell, Bryan Matheson, Beatrice Mason and Alan James Watson.

Judy Campbell, Norman Hudis, Dilys Laye, Peter Rogers, the late Joan Sims and Barbara Windsor gave me essential first-hand accounts of Hawtrey in action; Terry Johnson, Wendy Richard and Ned Sherrin answered my queries; and for their friendship and encouragement over many years I wish to thank Gyles Brandreth; Craig Brown and Frances Welch (whose brother, Nick Welch, is the source of this book's most egregious anecdote); Jonathan Coe; Peter Evans; Bevis Hillier; Barry Humphries; Philip Kemp; and Steve Masty. This book's dedicatees were my chief collaborators. Their mother, the Educational Psychologist Anna Lewis, endured a summer of double-entendre and Widdle jokes with reasonable fortitude.

Printed and manuscript material (much of it yellowing and crumbling) was consulted and gathered from the following sources – and I express my gratitude to the named individuals for their assistance: the BBC Written Archives Centre (Susan Knowles, Senior Document Assistant); the British Film Institute National Library; the National Film and Television Archive (Graham Melville, Cataloguer); the Special Collections Unit at the BFI (Janet Moat, Manager); User Services at the BFI (Nicole Fries, Periodicals Librarian); the Raymond Mander and Joe Mitchenson Theatre Collection

(Richard Mangan, Administrator); and the Theatre Museum, Covent Garden (Mel T. Christoudia, Curatorial Assistant).

Roger Lewis,
Hallowe'en 2000

The author and Faber and Faber wish to thank the BBC Written Archives Centre for permission to quote from previously unpublished copyright material in its possession; HarperCollins Ltd. for permission to reprint an extract from *The Kenneth Williams Letters* (edited by Russell Davies, copyright © The Estate of Kenneth Williams, 1994); and the Special Collections Unit at the British Film Institute's National Library for access to Gerald Thomas's production files, press books, publicity materials and Pinewood Studios ephemera.

Photographs courtesy of Mander & Mitchenson Theatre Collection, BFI/Canal+, Pinewood Studios (© Carlton International), Rex Features and *East Kent Mercury*.

Every effort has been made to trace copyright holders but if any have been inadvertently overlooked or omitted the author and publishers will be pleased to make the necessary arrangements at the first opportunity.

PART ONE

Art

Art

All these adults being infantile and concerning themselves with pirates and treasure (*Jack*), pistols and scimitars (*Up the Jungle*) camping trips and toilet jokes: it works because the acting is whole-hearted, as in an old-fashioned pantomime. The cast members seem to have the ability to fool themselves – there are no crappy post-modernistic ironic quotation marks around their performances, as there are clustering around Alexei Sayle, Julian Clary and Rik Mayall in *Columbus*, the ill-fated attempt to relaunch the *Carry Ons* in 1992. In the original series, Hawtrey, for instance, far from being literally or metaphorically oblique, is in very sharp outline. He sticks out; he stands out. He's always wearing peaked caps or plumed hats. He'll carry a rapier cocked at a gallant angle. His movements are full of sharp gestures. He's abrupt and angular and you'll find yourself watching him because his reactions, his responses, are quicker than anybody else; his over-eagerness is funny. Hawtrey wins us over, and creates his singular sort of atmosphere, under a heaven that is primary coloured and unrestrained. We see real streetscapes and fields (Slough, Maidenhead, the Pinewood Studios Car Park*), but the

---

So was the Ezra Pound of *Blast!* and the Edwardian youths who went off to that awfully big adventure in France. So was Orson Welles, who had the mind of Sherlock Holmes (another Peter Pan) and the body of Watson. I could go on – it ought to be a big book (with tie-in television series); there's Joe Orton doing Peter and Hook at his RADA audition: 'I think I was both at the same time – a schizophrenic act.' There's the sensibility of Maurice Sendak or the feyness of Mark Rylance. Suffice it to say that childishness – or childlikeness – is at the heart of the great art I personally admire, even if it is often won at the cost of a misbegotten child's tantrums, egotism and loneliness.

* Minutes from the pre-production meetings for each film contain information about the schedules and locations; to leaf through these records is like revisiting a vanished world – one is filled with a nostalgia for Betjeman's Metroland, that 'beckoned us out to beechy Bucks'; or it's like taking the red electric train 'gaily into Ruislip gardens' to our 'lost Elyseum of rural Middlesex': the Odeon

5

lewdness and fatuousness of the *Carry On* characters'
behaviour is artificial, stylized, exaggerated. The gag in
Cowboy, for example, is that Hawtrey's diminutive Red
Indian, Big Heap, has fathered the giant haystack that is
Bernard Bresslaw's Little Heap. Big Heap also speaks in
impeccable Received Pronunciation (and I should say that I
always find Hawtrey's distinctive voice, which was rather
smoked and warm, almost seductive). Or in *Doctor*, he's Mr
Barron and spends virtually the entire film flat on his back in
bed, suffering from a phantom pregnancy. His grimaces and
stoicism, as he is beset by labour pains, have (as Lamb would
say) 'no reference whatever to the world that is'; or consider
Hawtrey's hair, the jet black helmet which never changed
throughout his career, the fronds of his barnet hanging like
flax on a distaff. But the point is: Hawtrey seemed always to
be delightfully oblivious of his effects. He didn't appear
to know how outlandish he was. Take, for example, this

Cinema, Uxbridge, the Red Lion Public House, Iver, the Maternity Wing at
Heatherwood Hospital, Ascot, Chobham Common, Surrey, Adelaide Square,
Windsor, Denham Village, the Car Park Balcony of the Royal Lancaster Hotel,
Maidenhead; and there can't be a corner of Slough (where Betjeman wanted the
friendly bombs to fall) that the *Carry On*s didn't use. Once they went to
Camber Sands, near Hastings, for *Follow That Camel* ('a marquee would be
erected for lunch breaks on the car park adjacent to the Royal William. A
smaller marquee for serving tea breaks would be placed on the job'); and for
Convenience they went to Brighton ('the unit would stay at the Royal Albion
Hotel which is situated opposite the pier. It may be necessary to "double-up" in
twin-bedded rooms with private baths').

These place names and suburbs, the evocation of the South Coast's seaweed
tang and what Orwell called 'the huge peaceful wilderness of outer London'
may make me yearn for a former era, but Hawtrey wasn't so sentimental. 'We
went on location just *once* in the entire series and that was only as far as
Snowdon,' he said bitterly in 1988. For *Up the Khyber*, the location was at
Beddgelert and the Vicar, the Rev. D. Emrys Jones, kindly granted them
permission for the use of the church hall as a changing room, for the period
Sunday 19 May to 26 May 1968 inclusive, provided a contribution was made
to the parish funds.

introductory dialogue from *Spying* – an exchange between Hawtrey and Kenneth Williams:

– Name?
– Bind.
– James?
– No. Charlie.
– Number?
– Double O O.
– O what?
– Nothing. They just took one look at me and said 'Oh! Oh! Oh! . . . '

He began his career, needless to say, in *Peter Pan*. This was the original production, overseen by J. M. Barrie himself, which was revived annually at the Palladium and starred, in 1931, when Hawtrey was First Twin, Jean Forbes-Robertson as Peter and George Curzon as Hook. Five years later, when Hawtrey had been promoted to Slightly, Noël Coward's old role, Peter and Hook were played by that formidable married couple, Elsa Lanchester and Charles Laughton. Given his Bligh and Quasimodo, his gallery of grotesques and hams, Laughton must have been the definitive Hook, a roistering villain in velvet and ruffs, like his Henry VIII; glowering, vindictive, a Restoration dandy gone to the bad. Lanchester's Peter, according to James Agate, was 'not elfin but eerie, like some little boy cut off in the blossom of his youth'. With the green make-up, the character must have resembled a son of the bride of Frankenstein – and what dark shadows Laughton and Lanchester will have cast between them. Peter is the spirit of mischief and petulance; Hook is the nightmare father-figure – he's what Mr Darling becomes in your dreams; he's what the psychopathic Peter Pan is halfway to being already.

As a critic who looked in on a Thursday matinee commented, 'there was more than a touch of the sinister in this Peter ... indeed, I wondered whether Miss Lanchester thought she was playing Hook, so balefully did her eyes glitter'. The critic continued: 'The Lost Boys are splendidly male and spirited (what an improvement it was to have real boys in these parts instead of girls!) and Charles Hawtrey, as Slightly, shows a comedy sense not unworthy of his famous name.'

What's this? Charles Hawtrey – as in Sir Charles Hawtrey, born 1858, the son of an Eton housemaster, and who died in 1923, an actor-manager eulogized by Somerset Maugham ('with his magnetic personality, his incomparable humour and unfailing charm, he was a great comedian')? Is this the chap? The one who discharged his debts with his baccarat winnings and who blew his fortune on the gee-gees?* According to *What a Carry On: The Official Story of the Carry On Film Series*, our Charles Hawtrey 'was born in November 1914, the son of the light-comedy actor-manager, Sir Charles Hawtrey, who was celebrated for his immaculate man-about-town roles and won his knighthood for services to the theatre. Charles Hawtrey is immensely proud of his father and when he is in the mood delights in telling anecdotes about him. Well into middle age he was still billed as Charles Hawtrey Jnr, in deference to his father's memory.' Yet none of this is so.

The man who was Private Widdle will have enjoyed disseminating this disinformation – spinning these outright fibs about an illustrious forebear, as if he was John Gielgud explaining his links with the Terrys and the Beerbohm Trees.

---

* On his death his estate was valued at £1,180. It would have been even less, had not his wife, Katharine Elsie Robinson Clarke, a vicar's daughter, attempted to take him in hand.

Art

For who was going to bother to check up? The fact is, *our* Charles Hawtrey was born George Frederick Joffre Hartree on 30 November 1914 in Middlesex, the son of William John Hartree and Alice Crow. His father was an engineer – though whether this meant he was a sanitary engineer, or an inventor like Brunel, or whether he simply mended motor cars or mangles, I've no idea. But for a Hartree to have been mistaken for a Hawtrey wouldn't have hurt (Alec Guinness got his first engagements because he was assumed to be a scion of Lord Iveagh's brewing dynasty); and that the link was made public during a notice of *Peter Pan*, which is all about the psychology of fathers, sons and mothers, would thrill the Viennese Delegation. The person whom the original Hawtrey did directly influence, however, was Noël Coward. Like our Hawtrey, Coward had been a child actor – and like our Hawtrey, he was born into lower-middle-class pretension and semi-impoverishment in a London suburb, Coward being raised in Teddington, Hawtrey, though he'd still have been Wee Georgie Hartree then, in Hounslow.*

Sir Charles's money-spinners are wholly forgotten now: *Saucy Sally*, *A Message from Mars*, *Lady Huntsworth's Experiment*, *Please Help Emily* . . . Coward and his mother used to cadge tickets for the matinees, and the future Sir Noël would badger the actor at the stage door or in the wings. 'Go away, boy, for God's sake leave me alone!', he is reputed to have been told. But Coward was obsessed: he adored the acting which didn't look like acting; the naturalism. He was learning how to use his arms and hands; how to laugh on stage; how to produce actions and come out with

---

* Had Wee Georgie Hartree been of a military mind, instead of a waifish actor, he may have played upon the Joffre connection and alleged that he was the son of Joseph Jacques Césaire Joffre, Commander-in-Chief of the French Army during World War One.

lines that were so practised as to appear spontaneous. He was eventually cast by the master (or 'the guv'nor', as Coward called him) in his production of *Where the Rainbow Ends*, a lavish children's show which ran at the Holborn Empire each Christmas for forty years, in direct and deliberate competition with *Peter Pan*.

It sounds like dreadful, sub-Barrie-esque whimsy, but without Barrie's phantasmal, sad undertones. 'The idea is that where the rainbow ends is the place where heaven kisses earth, where all lost loved ones are found,' the programme notes explained. 'All who would reach that fair land must first pass through the country of the Dragon unless they find Faith's magic carpet to bear them on their way.' The Dragon is slain eventually by St George, in a patriotic pageant, and the orphan heroes, Vera, Crispian and Rosamund Carey, 'who are in the keeping of a hard and cruel uncle and aunt', somehow triumph. (It sounds like a proleptic Narnia.) In a clipping I found at the Theatre Museum, the audience was to be assured that 'nearly the whole of the company consists of children, very talented and well trained most of them, but still children' – amongst whom, in 1927 and 1928, was the teenage Hawtrey. Cast as one of the dozens of Flower Fairies, Dragon Flies, Water Lillies, Moths, Bats, Elves, Hyaenas, Mice and Frogs, he also understudied William the Page Boy, Coward's former role.

The throng of tots and pubertal players was supplied by Miss Italia Conti's drama school, founded by the ballet mistress in 1911. (The offices were in Great Ormond Street, excruciatingly opposite the Hospital for Sick Children.) Hawtrey attended for three years, paying his way with the fees received from playing an Arab in *The Windmill Man*, a White Cat in *Bluebell in Fairyland*, and the Boy Babe in *Babes in the Wood* at the Theatre Royal, Exeter. (Thirty shillings for six performances a week. Two and sixpence for pocket money. Five shillings for fares. Any balance to be put in a Post Office account by the Contis.) A classmate was Betty Marsden, with whom nearly half a century later he was to share a tent in *Camping*. 'When I was ten I auditioned for the drama school, Italia Conti,' she recalled. 'I met Charlie Hawtrey there. He may have been about nineteen then, but he never looked more than three.'

Sir Charles was several years dead by now; and who knows if the young Hawtrey saw him perform? But it was still his version of *Where the Rainbow Ends* that he appeared in and, though there were no blood-ties, they were kindred spirits nonetheless. John Gielgud, for instance, recalled Sir Charles's 'infinite charm and regretful pathos . . . Everything [he] did on the stage was perfect' – particularly his 'airy effect of enjoyment and leisure when he acted, passing off an embarrassing situation, eating a stage meal, or galvanizing undistinguished dialogue'. Aren't the *Carry On*s right there? The ropey lines, the daft plots, the clumsy use of props and stage business? There's an ease about Hawtrey, despite the quality of the films he was in; he's not spiky, nervy, brittle, like Kenneth Williams.* With his little skips and trips, and in his insect grace, he's benign. This is what I meant by saying he stayed a child actor for seventy years. There's no loss of innocence – no sense of injury, as with

---

* Williams returned to the *Carry On*s like a fanatical puritan or penitent needing his scourge. His *Diaries* are filled with complaints about how they chipped away at his self-esteem and talent. 'The scripts [are] schoolboy scatology . . . the most depressing sort of would-be funny rubbish' (14 May 1987). Time and again he vows to abandon the series and is plunged into a fit of melancholy ('I wonder how much of this present feeling of despair I can actually take?' 6 August 1964). Yet as he appeared in no fewer than twenty-five instalments, he was clearly drawn back masochistically. He took a perverse pleasure in the abasement, or (his choice of word) *ineptitude*.

Williams, whose performances (and whose personality) were over-deliberate, snickering and apopleptic. Both Hawtreys transcended their material.

Coward recalled the Italia Conti Schools having to rehearse in the damp basement of the Bay Malton Hotel, Great Portland Street, 'a great troupe, all those fairies and elves and frogs and caterpillars, gauntly escorted either by Miss C. herself or her sister, Mrs Murray' – Bertram Murray, her brother-in-law, being the Stage Manager and fond of astrakhan coats. Coward, it has to be said, knocked himself out to be rid of the pond life. (When Sir Charles wanted him to double William the Page Boy with a hyena or mouse, his mother vetoed it: you couldn't have a speaking role, then vanish into the crowd.) His career was a successful attempt to exact in reality what Sir Charles conveyed in the theatre. 'The silk would never be creased,' as Gielgud explained, 'the wheels would revolve with infallible precision.' Hence the ocean liners and riviera terraces, the Swiss chalets and Jamaican villas. Coward consorted with the Royal Family and, in 1984, a plaque was unveiled by the Queen Mother in Poets' Corner, Westminster Abbey. On stage and off, he represented sophistication and glamour. Hawtrey, who if anything represented impishness and quasi-innocent slap and tickle ('I work at the Butch Cassidy gymnasium ... I service the men's equipment'), and whose string vests and crome-yellow sou'westers could be a direct parody of Coward's dressing gowns, has a plaque in the Pinewood Hall of Fame, unveiled by Leslie Phillips.

Hawtrey never left Hounslow – except for his ignominious retirement to Deal, a town on the Kent coast, opposite the Goodwin Sands. He never mixed with the rich and famous. Where Coward turned his back for ever on the Lyons' Corner House ('macaroni and tomato sauce fourpence, a roll a penny, and a penny for the waitress'), Hawtrey would always dine frugally in canteens and department stores. Coward recalled trooping round the agencies, looking for work and representation ('I passed hours in those horrid waiting rooms'), Hawtrey never felt secure enough to stop touting for work and recognition. He never stopped being strange and solitary – he was beyond eccentricity.

From the luxury of his hotel suites, Coward remembered the dread Miss Conti dosing her charges on Epsom Salts, 'doubtless in the belief that the root of all evil lay in the bowels. But this only succeeded in making rehearsals extremely convulsive.' I don't know about the root of all evil, but to Talbot Rothwell, writer of the *Carry On*s, and to Peter Rogers and Gerald Thomas, the producer and director respectively, the bowels were the root of all humour. (When Hawtrey's Charlie Muggins, in *Camping*, pitches his tent in the army firing range and the mortar shells blow off his sleeping bag, he exclaims, 'I knew I shouldn't have eaten those radishes.') *Nurse*, *Doctor*, *Again Doctor* and *Matron* virtually make a fetish of the bed-pan and the bed-bath. *Convenience* entirely concerns a lavatory factory, W. C. Boggs & Son. The film was entitled *Carry On Round the Bend* for foreign export releases. Coward's creatures, Amanda and Elyot in *Private Lives*, or Garry Essendine in *Present Laughter*, sipping cocktails in their immaculate evening attire and being charming, seem worlds away. Which they are.* Coward's work is about success and its

---

* I mustn't give the impression, however, that Coward was continuously up in the empyrean. He had a saving vulgar streak a mile wide. Of an actress (Who? Edith Evans?) mistiming her lines in *After the Ball*, his adaptation of *Lady Windermere's Fan*, Coward said, 'She couldn't get a laugh if she pulled a kipper out of her cunt.' When, a little later in the scene, the audience began to titter, he added, 'She's just pulled it out.'

material trappings. The *Carry On*s are resplendently ordinary and makeshift. So what do they reveal of the British temper or sensibility? They are about, I think, pokey small-town Englishness (all those locations in Windsor, Slough or Brighton); they are about our idea of failure as success – that happiness is to be found in small things: a plot of garden where you can grow vegetables; a suburban fitted kitchen (Joan Sims' and Dilys Laye's homes in *Camping* are period pieces); caravan holidays; charabanc tours. The moral of *Abroad*, where they all go to the resort of Els Bels, where the hotel is still a building site and where it rains, is that it would have been better to have stayed at home.

Hawtrey and Coward were both highly mannered artistes, of course, and quite inimical. They lived concealed lives – the homosexual's fear of ostracism and exposure requiring masks and imposture; but Hawtrey didn't possess Coward's stately social confidence and overwhelmingness – nor his ambition and versatility (plays, songs and cabarets, as well as acting). Though he could be aloof and snooty, Hawtrey could never ape a solid patrician presence and be a ramrod-stiff-upper-lip naval captain in an equivalent of *In Which We Serve*; he lacked (in every sense) Coward's weight. Yet nor could Hawtrey be brazen and sentimental, as Coward was. Hawtrey was dainty, filigree, fastidious. (I'm talking exclusively about his performances – for in real life, had you been passing beneath his window in Deal, you'd have over-head him exhorting his partner to 'Come on and give it to me, big boy. Slap your bollocks against my arse!') Both he and Coward, however, had a distinctive face and voice; they shouldn't have been affecting (or of such fair proportions) but somehow were. Irresistibly bright and clipped, they could also intersperse their words and sentences with hummings, sighs and groanings. (Their essence was that they were full of laughter.) Their style – their tone and intention – was deliberately camp.

Where Sir Charles was polished, Coward was smooth (a different thing); and Hawtrey, going beyond the pair of them, was in a forthright epicene realm all of his own. The more I watch him, the more I'm aware of the spell of riot spreading inside him. I don't mean his sword-fencing episodes in *Don't Lose Your Head* or the way he pelts the police with fruit in *Abroad*, though there he's cherishably delinquent. I'm thinking of the way, wherever he is situated in a scene, that he'll contrive to glance or stare into the camera – or perhaps it is more accurate to say that he's gazing into the audience. He catches your eye; there's a collusion as he pirouettes into place and gives his secret smile. What's blissful is that he'll always be the same. (He doesn't age.) He never needed to alter his performance much – it's all a variation on his look of surprise, of wariness. He comes on, peers ever so slightly to the left and to the right, and makes his greeting: 'Oh, hello!' It's the simplest catchphrase in the world, and glitters with mischief. As Norman Hudis, who wrote *Sergeant*, *Nurse*, *Teacher*, *Constable* and *Regardless*, said to me: 'Hawtrey was an odd one – no doubt about that. But whether he was playing the eccentric or capitalizing on what oddities he had to create a persona, we'll never know.' Except perhaps we can.

He seems shy, and I'm always interested in shyness in an actor because it is a contradiction in terms. If you were lucky enough for him to agree to give an autograph, he wouldn't sign his name there and then – in full view – in the street. He'd gather up people's autograph albums, take them away, to be returned to the stage door later. He'd make such a meal of this. (It is like not wanting to be watched talking on the telephone.) Hawtrey, his campery outranked only by

Quentin Crisp, breaks the cardinal rule of camp in that he doesn't feel artificial; there's no (evident) striving after effects. Yet he only appears to be submissive. When he's in the army, the constabulary, MI6 or sitting on a hospital board (in *Again Doctor* he's a consultant surgeon: 'I do not object to jiggery but I do take exception to pokery') he mocks the very idea of power. He does this by being languid, unembarrassed, in his string vests and bobble hats, his askew perukes and jerkins a size too big. Though a loner (his characters are always bachelors and lodgers, never family men or men of property), he's not benighted; his is a 'natural isolation', to use Tynan's phrase about Michael Redgrave. He seems free of shame. He is a self-contained actor who doesn't really belong in the comedy of catastrophe, the comedy of fluster. In *Regardless* he is made to fall down the cellar steps (twice) and tumble into a bubble bath at the Ideal Home Exhibition. But curiously he's unlikely to come a cropper as he's so fleet of foot, so light and nimble, his face as grey and silver as a winter vision. Hawtrey mastered the great comedians' art of not doing anything; of being busy doing nothing. Eric Morecambe, Tommy Cooper, Jack Benny: they are hysterical just standing there, being still. There's a banishment of strain and effort – and of course Coward (and beyond him Wilde) made such apparent indolence into a philosophy, where 'Everybody was up to something, especially, of course, those who were up to nothing.'*

There was a strange interlude at the gala dinner held at the Savoy in 1969 to celebrate Coward's seventieth birthday. Laurence Olivier was called upon to speak, and as his tribute

---

* Compare Hawtrey with Bernard Bresslaw, for example. Bresslaw, at six foot seven inches, could either black up as a savage and roar and glower, or he could be the dope next door, with a cooing, sucking-dove voice. But when he doesn't have any lines to say, he disappears – he doesn't register, for all his size.

grew more convoluted and histrionic ('My dear Noëlie, I give you my love'), he broke off to cry, 'Help, Charles Hawtrey, help!' To whom was he making this appeal? Sir Charles had been dead for nearly half a century. Saving the odd theatre historian, few in the audience would have made a connection with Coward's mentor and early days; everybody will have thought he meant Sir Charles's other apprentice and namesake, the man who was at that moment in the nation's Odeons as Tonka the Great, 'King of Lovers, Father of Countless', in *Up the Jungle*. It's not too far-fetched a conceit.* Hawtrey strutting into the Savoy ('Oh, hello!') would have stopped the show – and anyway they did know each other, Larry and Charlie. Purring to Pinewood in his Rolls (to play the Mahdi in *Khartoum* or Wellington in *Lady Caroline Lamb* – sources differ), Olivier noticed a wispy figure, carrying a plastic bag filled with lemonade bottles and cigarettes, trudging along the road from Uxbridge tube station. He stopped the car and gave Hawtrey a lift to the studio.

'Larry tells me that he thinks it's outrageous that we get so little money for these films. He knows how much they make. We get no cars sent for us, no luxuries at all. My dears, Larry told me that he would not stand for such treatment!'

'That's why they don't cast him,' retorted Kenneth Williams (or Joan Sims – sources differ). The tawdriness of the *Carry On*s and the maltreatment of the cast would

* Though in fairness I should mention that in *Confessions of an Actor* ('The Autobiography of the Greatest Actor of Our Times'), Olivier writes, 'The 1920s brought forth a generation of actors, to which I belonged, who fell under the magical influence of the "natural" actors, led by Charles Hawtrey and Gerald du Maurier [who created the role of Captain Hook]. They deceived us into believing that realistic acting . . . was realistic behaviour; those marvellous actors hoodwinked us.'

become a big issue later on.* I'd give a lot, though, to know what else Olivier and Hawtrey talked about. They'd have had Jack Hawkins in common – Hawkins had been a choirboy and had known Olivier at All Saints', Margaret Street; Hawkins was then the Elf King in *Where the Rainbow Ends*, sharing the bill with Hawtrey, with whom he was a pupil at Italia Conti. Carmen Dillon, who in 1949 had won an Oscar for her set designs on Olivier's *Hamlet*, had also been the art director for the early *Carry On*s, *Sergeant* and *Cruising*. Olivier had been in *Private Lives* and knew Coward; and both he and Vivien Leigh knew Robert Helpmann, of whom more in a moment. Maybe nymphomaniacal Viv was a topic of conversation – for Hawtrey had co-starred with her at the Ambassadors Theatre in March 1937, in a 'Light Comedy' called *Bats in the Belfry*, about an old bag of an aunt who descends on a country vicarage to reorganize everybody's lives. Hawtrey and Leigh played Jerry and Jessica Morton, brother and sister. You won't believe this, but in the photographs that survive, Scarlett O'Hara and Private Widdle are credible siblings; and there is comedy in their poise, in their cultivated airs. Before he became anorexic and the colour of 'wry sour lemon acid' (Sylvia Plath), Hawtrey had a lissom appeal. (He and his stage sister look very young.) Leigh, who resembled, as everybody said, a porcelain shepherdess, always had a haunted inner-life, a morbid, camellia-strewn aspect which would one day win her an Oscar as Blanche du Bois; and at the very moment that *Bats in the Belfry* was running, she knew that Olivier was across the river, at the

---

* As a chap who'd fly down to the Côte d'Azur with his wife whilst a driver went on ahead with one of his classic motor cars, Peter Rogers, the producer, must be one of the world's champion ironists to be proud of the fact that when Kenneth Williams asked for transportation between his flat and Pinewood, 'that's when I had to draw the line . . . If he wanted a car it would have to come out of his fee' – which was £5,000 per film in 1958 and still £5,000 per film two decades later.

Old Vic, as Sir Toby Belch in *Twelfth Night*. Alec Guinness was Sir Andrew Aguecheek. But most importantly (for Leigh), Jill Esmond, Mrs Olivier, was Viola.

From the beginning of her clandestine relationship with Sir Larry, Leigh clung to illusions about love and gallantry, and the need to be protected, and this drove her mad. Hawtrey, too, had his disturbing, precarious side – and yet he never had any one great love in his life. 'There is so much cardboard in this business that one must take a long time before accepting people,' he'd argue, a guaranteed recipe for solitariness. With regard to his career, however, what I wonder now is why didn't Olivier invite Hawtrey to the National? Why wasn't Hawtrey at Chichester or in the Royal Shakespeare Company? He was born to play Sir Andrew Aguecheek; he *was* Sir Andrew Aguecheek, whose very walk was a jig, who delighted in masques and revels, who was a thin-faced knave. Hawtrey is the man Shakespeare had in mind when he came up with the character; he foresaw Hawtrey, his attributes and deportment, the 'brimstone in his liver' and his 'dormouse valour'. But it was not to be. Instead of appearing at Stratford or on the South Bank, Hawtrey spent the years of his *Carry On* fame, and after, touring in third-rate productions of *Dick Whittington* with the Patricia Comish Pantomime Babes; and had you been in the vicinity of the Pavilion Theatre, Torquay, for instance, in a summer of the early 1970s, you might have been tempted to book up and see him in a farce called *Stop It Nurse!*

This is intensely sad, a word that would often be used of him. In October 1966, Kenneth Williams recalled the wrap party for *Don't Lose Your Head*: 'One of the waitresses told me that Charlie Hawtrey asked her for a carrier bag full of left-over snacks from the buffet, to take home with him. The sadness of it all.' Joy Leonard, his neighbour in Deal, said, 'people wanted him to be like he was in the *Carry On* films, but on his own he became his true self – and so, often, he was just a sad little man.' Though he's almost impenetrably perky on camera, it is the case that Hawtrey's face lent itself to mournfulness. There was indeed a mystic sadness about him – and was he ever as ingenuous as he seemed? With the others in the *Carry On* team there's no question of mystery or teasing. (It's hard to think of them as particularly human, they are so lewd and loud.) Kenneth Williams, in particular, is an appalling actor, affected, caustic, shrieking like a peacock and with no sense of dramatic rhythm. Sinuous, snaky, serpentine, his voice and body coil and writhe across the screen, his forked tongue flickering, his nostrils looming and threatening to engulf you like railway tunnels. Williams was a talk-show star, a game-show panellist, an anecdotalist, a fully fledged character, with all that that entails, but in the *Carry On*s his showing off is reminiscent of amateur theatricals. I find him discomfiting. He's forced and hysterical – and that is not very lovable.

With Williams, everything about him is overstretched: the vowels, the neck muscles, the nostrils, the adenoids; the talent. There were no loose ligatures. It's overacting on an egregious scale, a baroque scale ('Infamy, infamy. They've all got it in for me!'). Even Coward was moved to comment, 'You are one of the few actors I know who can be outrageous and get away with it.' He's all sneers and cynicism, which is why he tended to specialize in uppity students or snotty professors whose tantrums and resentments mirrored or satirized his own real absence of heart. With Hawtrey, by contrast (and you are compelled to compare and contrast them because they are pitched together as a duo as often as not), there is a warmth. Williams, in art and in life, was

duplicating Helpmann's performance? As an artiste renowned for his excellence in a galliard or a coranto, and who could play on the viol-de-gamboys,* Helpmann brought to all he did, as those who remember him best as the child-catcher in *Chitty Chitty Bang Bang* will attest, a spidery elegance and charm. He also looked like a devil doll, ready to pounce. (He's a nightmare version of Hawtrey.) According to Guthrie, a riot erupted. 'The actors screamed their jokes, they fell from ladders, sat down in buckets of water, chased one another into cupboards, ran through the antic routine of farce.' Hawtrey wouldn't be as energetic as that again until he toured the provinces with *A Funny Thing Happened on the Way to the Forum* in the 1960s.

In a photograph that survives from the Old Vic, what is remarkable is Gremio's costume. It's out of a harlequinade, the flapping pockets, pleats and cuffs, the clown's slippers and enormous hat; it is fantastical. The make-up, too, is elaborate. The face is white as death, the silver beard and eyebrows: the Japanese Noh Theatre is restrained by comparison. Helpmann is also making a sweeping gesture. As a principal dancer and choreographer for the Sadler's Wells ballet, he can be seen playing a speaking role through mime, through the look of things – protuberant eyeballs, the curving of his hands. He's crystalline, pictorial – and Hawtrey picked up on that.

He himself, however, was never picked out again to appear in the classics, unless you include his Caterpillar in a radio production of *Alice in Wonderland*, broadcast on New Year's Day 1956. In March 1948, he had been engaged, at a

* Come on, those of you who did *Twelfth Night* for O-level: a *galliard* is an Elizabethan dance with a caper before the fifth step; a *coranto* is a rapid jig; a *viol-de-gamboys* was a medieval musical stringed instrument, played with a bow, from which the cello developed.

fee of ten guineas, to play Simon Tappertit in an adaptation of *Barnaby Rudge* on the Home Service, but at the last moment his part was deleted ('As, however, this is a definite booking and his contract is signed, I presume he will have to be paid,' the Drama Booking Manager, Miss Hewitt, grudgingly informed the Head of Programme Accounts, a Mr Riggs). The previous year he was to have appeared in Thackeray's *Pendennis*. The contract was signed and returned on 14 July. The very next day Miss Hewitt and Mr Riggs cancelled it. Hawtrey's letter of explanation to Hugh Stewart, the producer, dated 30 July 1947, is pitiful:

> I was extremely sorry not fulfilling my broadcast engagement last Sunday, and sincerely hope that you will forgive me. I had made arrangements to visit New York, but at the eleventh hour this had to be abandoned – I was unable to obtain an East-bound passage home, and this is necessary to comply with visa authorities. I do hope that you will pardon any inconvenience I have caused, I am very anxious to broadcast, and trust you will continue to bear me in mind when casting.*

I don't think he ever did make it to America; it was to be the career that never was. How he'd have agonized before walking out of a BBC job; how he'd have weighed the options. In the 1947 edition of *Radio Who's Who*, his declared ambition was 'To appear in American films made in California!' (He envisaged himself as a Charlie Chaplin or Stan Laurel, English comics who'd gone way out West.) So

---

* Stewart replied to this in the first week of August, saying how sorry he was 'to hear that you have been unable to make your visit to New York which must be most disappointing to you', and that he would let Hawtrey know 'as soon as a suitable date came up', which it strangely never did.

not only was there no further Shakespeare* – and no Restoration fops and dandies, no hooded serpents in Sheridan or Goldsmith, and no Dickens (save for a spoof Marley's Ghost in Thames Television's *Carry On Christmas*: 'I say – how much longer do I have to stand here moaning and clanging?'†): there was no Hollywood glamour coming in his direction, either. The BBC, in particular, categorized him as a juvenile and left it at that. Their archives, lodged at Caversham Park, near Reading, contain dozens of his contracts for *Children's Hour*. He appeared as Hubert Lane in many episodes of Richmal Crompton's *Just William* series throughout the 1940s, and with Patricia Hayes he was a boy detective in the long-running *Norman and Henry Bones*. (The instalments had titles like 'Mystery of Moulton's Fare', 'The Trunk Without a Key' and 'Secret Headquarters' and the series only petered out in 1960.)

Radio utilized less than the half of Hawtrey. To appreciate the full effect you'd have needed to see him in revue, a deliberately artificial form of live entertainment, long since rendered defunct by television. A smallish cast, a few songs, sketches, jokes, choruses, a dance or two; a medley. (I suppose it survives on the box as entertainments like *The Fast Show* or, going back a bit, *Not the Nine o'Clock News*. Lily Savage and Dame Edna are revue turns.) In 1938, he was at the Adelphi Theatre in Charles B. Cochran's *Happy*

---

* See, however, the Appendix, where Hawtrey claims he appeared in *Love's Labour's Lost* at the Haymarket Theatre in 1930, when he'd have been sixteen. I can find no record of that play being performed in London between an Old Vic production which opened on 8 September 1928 and another at the Westminster Theatre in the summer of 1932. Perhaps Hawtrey was in a one-off charity matinee, where an excerpt was given; perhaps he simply aggrandized his *curriculum vitae*. Whatever, he'd have been a peerless Moth, page to Don Adriano de Armado (whom he'd have been peerless as when older too).
† Broadcast on Christmas Eve 1969.

Returns. He appeared in scene vi, 'Things', the lyrics by Ira Gershwin, the music by Harold Arlen. I then can't find his name until the finale, 'Sunday in the Park', where he was a stallholder. Star of the show was Beatrice Lillie, who throughout the evening was draped in a variety of costumes by Schiaparelli. Hawtrey had more to do in *New Faces*, the one where he was Sir Andrew Aguecheek. He did a Tin Pan Alley number, 'Mother o' Mine', a spy drama sketch, 'Under Which Flag', and in 'The Gods Look Down' he was Zeus, which must have been a sight. The revue is still remembered for Judy Campbell's throat-tightening rendition of 'A Nightingale Sang in Berkeley Square', a song which, like 'Danny Boy', is about nothing and everything.

'I was doing a film – and if I came back early, or looked in on rehearsals, there'd be Charlie entertaining everybody doing my numbers, in full drag,' Judy Campbell, at eighty-five the sole survivor, recalls. 'I was so fond of him – we were so young; it was such a beautiful beginning – which makes it all the more tragic, the dreariness later, in Deal. I wish I'd known – I could've tried to find him, but we lost touch, as people do.'

New Faces ran twice nightly for a long time; at the Comedy, then a six-week tour around the army camps, then back to the Apollo, where rain poured from the bomb-damaged roof right on to the stage. 'Charlie was so good at doing my numbers, I said, "Have them." He was much funnier than I'd have been, and he grabbed them. So he did the Vivandière's song, which was meant to be mine ("Vivandière, with a bottle of brandy on my derrière"); and that's how they got to give me Eric Maschwitz's "Nightingale" instead, which stopped the show in a most extraordinary way. You see – it was the early years of the war, when we thought we were losing. There was this incredible atmosphere of danger and uncertainty – and of excitement. The air raids were on. The show was constantly interrupted by bombs falling. The cast and the audience would sometimes be marooned in the theatre until two in the morning. We'd invite them up on the stage to dance along with us. It's funny – up in the night sky, Hitler's bombers; down below, Charlie Hawtrey, with that beady face and huge specs, in a dress. One evening Noël Coward came to see me. "It's Noël Coward. May I come in?" I thought it was Charlie playing a joke. Another time, we all planned to go to the Café de Paris – the night it was bombed. We arrived in time to see people rushing across Leicester Square carrying buckets of water.'

The revue was recorded on acetate discs from microphones installed in a stage box. The BBC intended to broadcast some of the songs on C. B. Cochran's birthday; unfortunately, having survived the war, the case containing the fragile long-playing microgrooves fell off the back seat of a taxi, so that was that. The resultant splinters and shards thus belong with the larger drama of evanescence and the passage of time that has to encompass Keatsian nightingales, flimsy frocks and dancing in the dark.

In July 1941, Hawtrey joined the company of *The New Ambassadors' Revue*, described as 'mock-ballet, opera without music, sentiment and song', produced by Cyril Richards. Hawtrey's co-star was Ernest Thesiger, who 'romp[ed] through the show in many different costumes'. A song called 'How I Bust My Bust', where he was attired as a charlady, might be deemed a play on words. Hawtrey appeared with the venerable stick insect and erstwhile Doctor Praetorius ('Here's to a new world of gods and monsters!') in several sketches, one being a cod opera called 'Violetta', where the cast seem dolled up for *Romeo and Juliet*.

The following year, at the Vaudeville Theatre, in the Strand, was *Scoop!* Here's what *The Times* had to say:

The Man who was Private Widdle

Mr Henry Kendall leads an indomitably cheerful company through a vale of inanity . . . Mr Charles Hawtrey sometimes by sheer technical efficiency strike[s] out a spark or two . . . The dancing and the music may be described as bright, and that only seems to make the dullness of the dialogue worse.

For so much of his career Hawtrey was doomed to be a crack troop in crap. The French have Balzac's *La Comédie Humaine*; we have the *Carry On*s. Scandinavia had Ingmar Bergman and Italy Federico Fellini. We have Barbara Windsor's boobs popping out and her bra slapping Kenneth Williams full in the face ('OOOhh, Matron! Take them away!'). On some days I'm immensely proud and patriotic about this. Yet as much as we love the *Carry On*s, our affection isn't based on an appreciation of their artistic merits; and part of the pleasure (paradoxically – perversely) lies precisely in seeing these over-qualified actors (Hattie Jacques, Sid James and Terry Scott, as well as Hawtrey) cope with the directorial and scriptual atrocities, lifting flat dialogue or banal predicaments sky-rocketingly. Yet there's a sketch in *Scoop!* which suggests how chastening it must actually have been for Hawtrey. Henry Kendall played the Ogre of the Organ at the Odeon at Oundle, a pathos-steeped monologue revealing the feelings of the man who, day after day, has to churn out the treacly music that accompanies silent movies. What a lot of hatred must build up inside.*

* 'I know both what I want and what I might gain, / And yet how profitless to know, to sigh / "Had I been two, another and myself, / Our head would have o'er looked the world!"' (Browning). The sentiment is dramatized in Powell and Pressburger's *A Canterbury Tale* (1944), when Dennis Price, who earns his living playing the piano in cinemas, is permitted to give a recital on the cathedral organ. Hawtrey may be glimpsed exceedingly briefly in this film as a railway porter, blowing a whistle and waving a flag.

What a huge release, though, too, the world of revue. As for Dick Emery, Stanley Baxter or Barry Humphries (and Dougie Byng and Danny La Rue), Hawtrey could indulge in what he loved best, which was dressing up in furs and taffeta. He wasn't a drag artist exactly. He didn't remind the audience (as with a pantomime dame) that the voice is male, the body is male. He really did lose himself within the petticoats and corsets, the long black cotton gloves, make-up and jewellery. In *New Faces* he played Natasha, curvaceous in a leopard-spotted cocktail dress, who flirts with the dashing Helmuth (John Bentley) in an Austro-Hungarian operetta sketch. As the befrocked Vivandière (cheerleader), in 'Women and War', he was drawn by Feliks Topolski. In *The New Ambassadors' Revue*, he and Thesiger were 'War-Minded Females' in a sketch called 'The Amazons', about a pair of old dears preparing to deal with a possible Nazi invasion ('Give them my buns with strychnine in them'). In *Scoop!* he was the leader of a ladies' café orchestra ('Oh, Madame René, you're as good as Toscanini') and, with wild hair, Farola the Female Fakir:

> They can prod me with needles and prick me with a spear,
> And I show neither feeling nor fear;
> And once for a laugh,
> I was sawn up in half –
> I'm Farola the Female Fakir.

– which is I suppose a ditty about being indomitable, which is what comes across in Hawtrey's performances; his determination. He shows us how different he was. He's defiant about his girlishness. There are two moments in the *Carry On*s when this is apparent. In *Constable*, to observe suspected shoplifters, Hawtrey and Kenneth Williams disguise themselves as old ladies, Agatha and Ethel, and mingle with the crowd. First there's a scene in the toilets as they climb into their clothes. A look of pure bliss steals over Hawtrey as he slips into his twinset and adjusts his pearls ('I haven't done this since I was in the army – a camp concert'). Then, sauntering through the lingerie department, where Williams has to have trouble balancing on his high-heeled shoes, Hawtrey's feminine carriage is perfection – it's not over-done. You realize with a smile that he is completely in his element, and he glows.

The other transformation is in *Again Doctor*, where his character, Dr Ernest Stoppidge, spends much of the film wearing a powder blue skirt, sky blue ostrich plumes and zircon spectacle frames as Lady Puddleton, or Piddleton as Sid James has it. The plan is that, by pretending to be a woman, he can infiltrate Jim Dale's slimming clinic and steal the secret formula, a potion that comprises gnat's milk, banyan tree juice and powdered parrot droppings. But who cares about plans or plots? The appeal of the *Carry On*s, like revue, was that they weren't constrained by stories or narratives. People go camping, or into hospital, or call a taxi, or find themselves in a jungle set or a maharaja's palace set; it's pretty random. In a sense, nothing happens in these films except, where Hawtrey was concerned, chances are engineered for him to burlesque the idea of virility and manhood: in *Doctor*, where he's allegedly pregnant; in *Up the Jungle*, where he's keeping tribes of women happy; in *Cleo* or *Don't Lose Your Head*, where he's pawing the girls and shoving a hand up their knickers. Even as a child, when I first saw him in *Camping* at Bedwas Workman's Hall, I knew that he was completely wrong; that there was something amiss with this effeminate creature's sexual innuendos. 'She's been showing me how to stick the pole up!' he said, emerging from his tent with Valerie Leon.* He mocked machismo by being randy and looking androgynous.

If Hawtrey's work has any tale to tell it's this: that he was never more himself than when playing a woman. 'As you know,' he crowed to the casting people at BBC television service in 1946, 'my make-up is unbelievable, and my wardrobe very smart, so what more do you want?' (What indeed?) When shooting was completed on *Again Doctor*, he wrote a rare letter to Peter Rogers, the producer:

> Thank you for your wonderful luncheon party at the Mirabelle yesterday [i.e. 2 May 1969] – the food – the wines – the company – all of which seemed so appropriate after what was generally agreed to be *the* happiest production. Whilst you remained, undeniably, our gracious host, you complimented us, not to say delighted, by being one of our motley lot.
>
> With love from
> Your exported† but never let it be said rejected
> *Charles Hawtrey*

Nobody believed him when he said he enjoyed wearing a dress only because he had a case of boils on his bum and the loose frock allowed air to circulate, though it is true that a costume girl found him with the skirt over his head and

* The wretched John Trevelyan, secretary of the British Board of Film Censors, had insisted on a redubbing of the original, superior line, 'She's been showing me how to stick my pole up'!

† *Exported*? Hawtrey's use of this word is explained by referring to the minutes of the pre-production publicity meeting, held on 1 September 1966, for *Don't Lose Your Head*:

> . . . overseas papers would be very interested in Charles Hawtrey who had made his mark already in overseas markets in 'Carry On' pictures. For this reason good [stills] pictures of Hawtrey would help identify him with the film and earn greater publicity.

he was smearing ointment on his anus – but that could mean anything. The humour with the Lady Puddleton impersonation is that he's virtually the same as ever – the little sideways glances, the little sniffs and sighs. Hawtrey is Hawtrey and he's having a lot of fun. He'd have liked to have had more. Having read the script of *Follow That Camel* he wrote by return to Gerald Thomas, the director:

> I was so glad to chat with you to-day. There is little one can do about the role of 'Le Pice' – but the part of Batman of Beau [Simpson] gives a real opportunity of being funny. I can only hope that Peter [Rogers] can be persuaded to give this part to me – and am certain that both you and he would not regret so doing.*

Simpson was played in the event by Peter Butterworth. So it's Butterworth, plump and jocund, who had the pleasure of dressing up in Angela Douglas's bridal gown to be chased around the harem. Hawtrey's Le Pice, an adjutant in the Foreign Legion, who swishes along in the sand and twirls in and out of the fort, resplendent in crimson breeches and white gloves, is nevertheless one of my favourite performances. With his brass buttons sparkling and the silver fringes of his epaulettes shimmering, he is in a rhythm so very much of his own. But Hawtrey doesn't have much to do or say. In the main he stands about in the middle distance, listening and waiting, whilst Phil Silvers chortles and mugs, Kenneth Williams compares nostrils with a dromedary and Jim Dale, rather tiresomely, dithers and drops his rifle. Hawtrey, attentive and twinkling, does a lot of acting with his eyeballs.

He could always transcend limitations and in many a *Carry On* he's no longer an actor, he's no longer a performer.

* 23 March 1967.

He's more than that – he's a manifestation. Everything about him – his bony witch's fingers, his round spectacles, his skin which was like tracing paper, his coal-black lock of hair – was picturesque; it's the stylization of a silent movie. He's like a drawing by Beardsley or Cocteau, a sketch in pen and ink, a few contours and curlicues, held together by nervous tension. This is particularly true of *Doctor*: he's like the sheeted dead, as immobile on his hospital cot as the effigy on a tomb. Frankie Howerd is braying and oo-err-missuss-ing in the foreground, but it is Hawtrey, in pointed profile, oblivious to the world in the background, who is funny. The way his pyjamas are done up to the topmost button is funny.

I can't think of anyone else who could wear clothes like he did. In *Spying*, he wears cycling shorts, cap and goggles for creeping about Vienna, a gendarme's uniform when mingling in Casablanca, and a large trench coat, which hangs around him like a ballgown of Scarlett O'Hara's, when he's at large on trains and planes. In *Convenience*, where he's the industrial designer of toilet seats and water closets, he goes in for long tangerine and shocking pink cravats, orange paisley shirts and a purple fedora. He's at his most surreal – or mannered – in *Abroad*, appearing in a striking array of blouses, trilbies and mullion-patterned trousers. Leaving the hotel for a day at the beach, he carries a ball, a lilo and a multi-coloured carpet bag. He also puts on a face mask, as protection from the sun.

It's not that he was an exhibitionist (though he was – actors are); it's more that, by slightly tilting a hat brim, or swishing a stick, or holding and flapping a pair of gloves, Hawtrey could make all clothes look eccentric. With him, dress is fancy dress and what he's demonstrating is the fundamental nonsensicality of any attire that's not as strictly functional as the caveman's pelts. Caveman gear is much on view in *Cleo*, of course, amongst Kenneth Connor's burly British contingent. The Romans, led by Sid James, wear splendid breastplates and gold armour, acquired cheap when Peter Rogers bought the abandoned fixtures and fittings from the disastrous Elizabeth Taylor / Richard Burton production. Hawtrey, though, as Seneca, Caesar's father-in-law, is dressed in a simple brown jerkin which accentuates his feebleness, his peculiarity and absurdity. His matchstick arms and legs are in evidence and on his head there's a hilarious tea-cosy wig. In place of the dialogue he's not given he fills the soundtrack with a filthy laugh. The film contains one of Hawtrey's finest moments. Wanting to witness Cleopatra and Mark Antony commit intimacy, he hides in a large urn and totters along the corridors and hops up marble steps. Now and again he peeps out, the lid rising above his wig like a tam-o'-shanter. Here's a person who not only makes suits, uniforms and smart casuals comic; he makes pottery comic. The sequence demonstrates the paradox of this actor – that his affectations seem natural; or as Hazlitt would say, his 'folly is indigenous to the soil, and shoots out with native, happy, unchecked luxuriance'. He had no other spring of action, or motive of conduct, in his art, save displaying his bright plumage. Showing us he exists is enough. Hence, Special Constable Gorse, making his entrance in the police station carrying a bunch of carnations ('With a little snip here and another snip there. Snip! Snip!'); or Mr Timothy Bean, the music master in *Teacher*, immaculate in white tie and tails, like Malcolm Sargent, at the school concert, and getting splattered with paint; or Private Widdle's unfeasibly hairy sporran.

In *Loving*, he puts on a turban and a Sherlock Holmes cloak to snoop after Sid James, Sir Toby to his Sir Andrew, outside the Gents Lavatory at Windsor and Eton Central Station. In his office there is a primitive telephone. According to the Production Manager's memorandum about location facilities, the date for shooting such scenes was 13 May 1970. What I like about Hawtrey, however, is that he makes no attempt to exist in the modern world. Temperamentally he belongs in the previous century. Whilst the coxcombry of the *Carry On*s alludes to saucy seaside picture postcards, with their garishly printed vermilions and crome yellows, Hawtrey himself could be off a Toulouse Lautrec poster. He'd have fitted in with Montmartre café and boulevard life; the circuses and the music hall. His face, if you study it, is a sallow absinthe green. He looks like he's illuminated from below, by gaslight.

The *Carry On*s were a dreamworld, where no real adultery or fornication takes place (Kenneth Connor is always tormented by sexual frustration; Kenneth Williams is always fending off Hattie Jacques, or Patsy Rowlands' Freudianly named Miss Withering, to preserve his chastity). They are ribald but restrained. It's enough, in mid-twentieth century England, for gentlemen to realize that they can take their jackets off without civilization coming to an end. Sid James does a lot of ogling and cor blimey-ing, but I think the only time he gets anywhere is with Amanda Barrie's Nympho of the Nile – and then the censor cropped the post-coital pay-off scene 'So as to get rid of the suggestions that he is physically exhausted'. And when he jumps on her and the bed collapses, the shot had to be cut 'before we see him wriggling his legs'. In the *Carry On*s, despite the obsession with doctors and nurses, nobody is actually ill; hospitals are packed with people in rude health. Industrial disputes are settled by taking management and workforce on a coach trip to Brighton. When Sid James, Bernard Bresslaw, Peter

Butterworth or Kenneth Connor* dress up as women, to get in and out of some scrape, the effect is half-hearted on purpose – literally laughable and whooped-up.

Hawtrey is at odds with such a comic convention. His was a more serious illusion. The *Carry On*s were facile, 'a world of themselves almost as much as fairyland', as Lamb said about the plays of Congreve; but the point about Hawtrey – conveyed in his laughter, his wine-dark voice, his painted eyebrows – is that he implied a spirit of real perversity. His commitment to costume is far from silly or trivial, or at least it wasn't to him; and he could be shamelessly grotesque, like May Belfort cradling her kitten or Aristide Bruant barracking the audience in the Lautrec lithographs. I'd have given a lot, therefore, to have been at the Duke of York's Theatre on 15 August 1939 for the opening night of *Counterfeit!* by Cyril Butcher and Albert Arlen. Having to do with a Blackpool family, the Entwistles, coming up to London to take over a legacy in the shape of a murdered cousin's house in St John's Wood, 'humour abounds', said the *Marylebone Chronicle*. Before being topped, the cousin conceals a horde of banknotes behind a secret panel and the Entwistles vie with a gang of robbers, disguised as their servants, who extinguish the lights, and bang and crash like ghosts, to find the loot. Also wandering on to the premises is the Countess of Ellerdale, who gives Maggie Entwistle, a social climber, advice about mudpacks and boudoir caps. The slinky,

---

* What a pain in the arse he is. The only person I know who can abide Connor's going-to-pieces, swallowing hard, nervous-wreck act is Jonathan Coe, who wrote an entire novel on the subject, *What a Carve Up!* (1994). His *The House of Sleep* (1997) was filled with allusions to Billy Wilder's *The Private Life of Sherlock Holmes*, the Baker Street set for which at Pinewood was used for exterior views of the Hawtrey character's boarding house in *Convenience*. I await Coe's homage to *The Shoes of the Fisherman*, no doubt to be called *Kiss My Ring!*

provocative Countess in her high-necked evening gowns was played, according to the programme, by Charlotte Tree. The reviewer for *The Stage* was puzzled: 'Charlotte Tree's portrayal of the bogus Countess is as absurd as it is improbable, and her telephone conversation to Covent Garden is as funny as a turn in a variety entertainment. At the conclusion it appears that the Countess is in reality a boy played by Charles Hawtrey, but one is under the impression that the smart person who calls on the Entwistles is Charlotte Tree.'

Other people were quicker off the mark in spotting that Charlotte Tree and Charles Hawtrey were synonymous. Twenty years later, when asked for a résumé to include in the press release for *Constable*, these are the cherished notices Hawtrey copied out for the publicist:

> Mr Charles Hawtrey, if indeed it is him who flaunts a tiara at the opera, amazingly deceives most of us. *The Times*

> ... a genuine surprise in the revelation that a bogus countess was so bogus that 'she' was played by a man, Mr Charles Hawtrey. *Observer*

> I was taken in completely and hereby hand the biscuit to the person or persons concerned ... Charles Hawtrey. *Daily Telegraph*

Telling the tale of his seamless artifice, of how he'd taken in the world, including the saturnine Eric Portman, a homosexual from Halifax who was a great actor and nobody's fool, became Hawtrey's party trick – a set-piece which, no matter how many times she'd heard it, never ceased to enthral Hawtrey's mother. (The Oedipal implications of a mother's being transfixed by a son's transvestism is another one for the Viennese witch-doctors.) 'He'd wander in and out of the studios with his mother,' Joan Sims tells me, 'and on one occasion, in the middle of his story about playing a woman in this thriller in the West End, his mother, who'd been listening so intently, dropped her lit cigarette from her mouth into her open handbag, which started to smoulder. "Charlie! Your mother's on fire!" I yelled. All he did was pour her tea in the bag and snap it shut; and he carried on with his story without a hitch.'*

Hawtrey knew how to carry himself as a girl. With him it wasn't *La Cage aux Folles* lubriciousness or Denis Quilley in *Privates on Parade*: the papers praised Hawtrey's 'realism' and the *Daily Express* sent a photographer around to his dressing room for before-and-after shots of the make-up process: a weedy man becoming a languid elongated *femme*

---

* This anecdote, often told by Kenneth Williams, is dramatized in Terry Johnson's television drama *Cor Blimey!* The actor playing Hawtrey, however, Hugh Walters, whilst capturing the mannerisms, was far too plump for the role, despite having lost a stone and a half by (Johnson informs me) 'putting himself on a lettuce diet, leading to more sound-stage flatulence humour than I'd intended'. Samantha Spiro's Barbara Windsor, by contrast, is so spot-on – chirruping and warm-hearted – that when the real Barbara Windsor appears at the end, in a cameo, she was less convincing at being herself than the girl who'd impersonated her. The metaphysics (not to mention the hermeneutics) of why this should be so will vex me for ever.

Cor Blimey! was adapted by the author from his stage play, *Cleo, Camping, Emmanuelle and Dick*, which opened at the Lyttelton in 1998. Bringing the might of the National Theatre to bear on the shabbiness of the *Carry On*s – slavishly reproduced sets by William Dudley; tinny, scratchy monophonic music by Barrington Pheloung – seemed so ironic and post-modernistic it was all almost in the realm of kitsch.

Johnson's play (in both incarnations), a loving look at the darkness and despondency to be found behind the scenes, is brilliant and preposterous. He recreates and conveys the squeals, yells, giggles and howls of the cheap comedies to perfection. But he also gives Sid, Kenny and Babs over-eloquent, unlikely speeches about Art, Life and the Consolations of Philosophy, and these are all imposed on them – the author sounding off. They are saying things and debating things they'd never have thought, let alone spoken out loud, or to each other. But the play had a lingering cello note of sadness that I loved.

fatale. He was more than a man impersonating a woman; it's more as if the woman hiding inside him could now emerge. His secret could come out in performance – acting gave him that degree of freedom; and you begin to appreciate that behind his apparent imperturbability lay a darker ambience, a warped world of irrational needs, ambiguousness and sexual anxiety.

If Hawtrey was too late to join the ravaged cabaret artistes at the Moulin Rouge, the hermaphrodites painted by Charles Conder or the rubicund Londoners Phil May sketched for *Punch*, he did at least make one (fleeting) appearance in a neurotic masterpiece, Hitchcock's *Sabotage*, released in 1936 and based on Conrad's *The Secret Agent*. Charles Hawtrey and Alfred Hitchcock? An unlikely combination; but there he is nonetheless, in an atmosphere of espionage and danger. Verloc has a clandestine meeting at the echoey, shadowy aquarium in Regent's Park Zoo. His foreign contact is telling him he must plant a bomb that'll be timed to go off during the Lord Mayor's Parade. Who should go by but Hawtrey as a youth, telling his girlfriend about the reproductive habits of the oyster. 'After laying a million eggs, the female changes sex,' he exclaims. 'I don't blame her!' retorts his companion. It's a delicious piece of black comedy, heightening the mood rather than giving relief from it; and in the face of (or in the midst of) the Hitchcockian chiaroscuro, Hawtrey is fabulously blithe – as he was to be nearly forty years on, in *Convenience*, where, the sex life of crustaceans still on his mind, he announces, 'Let's all go on the pier and have a winkle.'

Bivalves transforming their gender; spies pretending to be one thing but actually being another; the double-crossing and treachery of espionage and counter-espionage; cross-dressing and transsexuality; female impersonation: Hawtrey was drawn to inversions and alterations, as he veered away from having to be an adult male. At war with masculinity, if he couldn't be a woman, he could at least retreat or dig in and be a boy for ever; and before he became enmeshed in the *Carry On*s, he was a foil in the films of Will Hay. If the *Carry On*s are puerile, Hay, who played a crabby schoolmaster, presided over an academy of preserved infants, a band of freaks with sharp or pert miniature features, slow of wit (Graham Moffatt) and toothless (Moore Marriott – who is normally the caretaker or sidekick). It's not a second childhood that's depicted, however – it's a disinclination (or disability) to leave the original one.

With titles like *Boys Will be Boys*, *Good Morning Boys* and *Dandy Dick*, you'd be forgiven for thinking that here's a corpus to be catalogued under *la haute pédérastie*. The boys in question, however, are ancient. (Hawtrey was twenty-eight when he made *The Goose Steps Out* in 1942). Indeed, in one of the films, the plot involves a gang of superannuated thieves hiding from the cops by infiltrating the classroom, putting on Eton collars and passing themselves off as ordinary pupils. This is not too impossible a premise. Nobody thinks to remark on the queerness of these broken noses, rheumy eyes, lumbering gaits and gruff voices because they are *all* wizened and puckered, like jockeys. These films, astoundingly popular in their day, are in fact the stuff that bad dreams are made of; they answer the question, whatever happened to the Lost Boys? They grew old but they didn't grow up.

Hay, who was born in Stockton-on-Tees in 1888, first came out with his schoolmaster sketch in 1909, so he's thus an authentic Edwardian music hall comedian, suffused with the sepia mists and twilight mood I associate with that era. The films, of course, are black and white – except no black and white film is ever black and white, so to speak. There's an infinity of greys and silvers, which particularly suit Hawtrey's El Greco face, his quixotic Blue Period Picasso face, his eyes constantly on the go, taking everything in. Thus he stands out in the Will Hay movies: he's the only one amidst the throng of withered Tweedledums, who can be natty and flip, who has the gravity and pride of a believable child. (He looks like Harry Potter.)

The rogueries of the pupils aren't very funny. Gambling and smoking don't look like premature pursuits with this lot; the joke goes for nothing. Why are these geriatrics fumbling with invisible ink and bothering to cheat in exams? The main gag, however, is the reversal of the master–schoolboy relationship. It's youth (i. e. Hawtrey) who tutors crapulous experience (Hay) and springs him from embarrassing situations, tricks and revels. I have to say, I think I hate Hay. The way he shouts all the time. The gruffness. The tetchiness. The scowling bemusement. The way he scratches his chin as he copes with one being put over on him – as convicts fleece him, as the cock-a-hoop pupils swindle him, as Hawtrey the swot pipes up, 'I've finished, sir, despite my handicap.' Mumbling and bumbling and saving us from Hitler, Hay, with his atmosphere of haste and trouble, shabby and out-at-the-elbows, does, however, possess one quality which is undeniably courageous: he's not aggrieved by our finding him unsympathetic.

Hawtrey was proud of his association, praising Hay's 'matchless professionalism' and for encouraging him 'to find the fine line between farce and comedy. It took me years of practice.' Is there such a line? Does the division or distinction make sense? Farce involves action; comedy can simply arise from the slightest gesture or glance, or from the ambient temperature. Were I a Will Hay fan, I'd argue that his look of surprise and his being taken by surprise are what is amusing. And I'd argue that the comedy of incompetence – of ditheriness and nervousness – which he may indeed have invented – is what culminates in Norman Wisdom, Basil Fawlty and Inspector Clouseau. These are all idiots who, despite themselves, succeed. (Though I realize now that Basil Fawlty never wins through; he's in a continuous paroxysm of fretfulness.) I'd perhaps even say that the descendants of Hay's role hardly rate as comic performances at all, as such. Their principal attribute is the preservation of dignity; thus our laughter is rather cruel, and degrading.*

So what did Hawtrey derive from *The Ghost of St Michael's* (made on Michael Balcon's finest Scottish castle set at Ealing) and the rest of them? I think far from discriminating between farce and comedy, he learned to make an elision. As the child outwitting the adults – as a child who is the mastermind – he combines elements of pantomime (animated gestures, a high clear voice capable of hooting with complaint) with a cocksureness, an eagerness, a pertinacity, above all a poise, that'll flower into his wax fruitiness later on. The germ or worm of his voluptuous campery is here: Charlie Muggins, in *Camping*, high-stepping it along the open road, his rucksack a-dangle with jangling pots and pans; or the keenness of Private Widdle, another innocent abroad; or his great hauteur as the Duc de Pommefrit, in *Don't Lose Your Head*. (Peter Rogers wrote to him saying, 'Dear Duke d'Hawtrey, No one else could play the Aristocrat': who'd he originally wanted to be? Joan Sims' blowsy Desirée Dubarry? The lady-in-waiting played by Valerie Van Ost?)

---

* I don't find Wisdom, Cleese or Sellers funny. I find Jerry Desmonde, Prunella Scales and Herbert Lom funny. But of course the comedy is set up by Norman, Basil and Clouseau acting the giddy-goat.

In the company of Hay and his homunculi, Hawtrey is spruce, dainty and astringent; he has a peculiar grace. These are alert, preening performances, as he outfoxes the Nazis in *The Goose Steps Out*, locates secret passages and outfoxes the Nazis (again) in *The Ghost of St Michael's*; and in *Good Morning Boys* he definitively incarnates a swot, his nose an inch from the exercise book. He's diligent and inspirational – and it is his keenness – his eagerness – to be a policeman, taxi driver, soldier, sailor or spy that'll animate him later on. In the early *Carry On*s he's made to be accident-prone (tipping tea, door-knobs coming off in his hand, smashing cars, etc.); but what seems weakness or effeteness is in fact intrepid. He's never a nincompoop in the way Hay was; the terrible teacher or railway stationmaster, nervously coughing and fidgeting because he's in the wrong job. He's robust.

Hawtrey had his own authority, and I'm uncomfortable (on his behalf) when scripts expose him to scorn and demand that he'll fall through a hole in the floor (*Teacher*), be drowned in a toilet bowl (*Screaming*), have rancid pea soup poured over his head (*Camping*), or be made to run for miles across a ploughed field until he's a dot in the distance (*Cabby*). It's as if they were doing their best to dent his cheerfulness and glee, but he had too much resource for that. (It's a paradox of camp that it seems ephemeral and made of tinsel; actually it'll be resilient and surprisingly impregnable.*)

---

* Look how the *Carry On*s themselves remain prevalent – permanently on sale at Woolworth's and on the box every single Sunday afternoon. They are popular and beloved; perhaps what we admire is that they *are* silly and trivial. Kenneth Williams, through the publication of his *Letters* and *Diaries*, has a permanent place in our literature. On other fronts, Danny La Rue used to growl baritonally, 'Don't let this wig fool you mate,' and threaten to clock any heckler. Oscar Wilde, ragged by hearties at Magdalen, physically flung them down the stairs.

The Man who was Private Widdle

He's a poignant actor, the more so because he was beset by brusqueness and humiliation. And it's his cheerfulness and glee that will survive of him, I think. When I picture the expression on that eggshell thin face of his, as he plays the piano, puts on women's finery, hops on a kiddie's scooter, polishes the brass taps and lays out the towels and cakes of soap by the basins (*Screaming*), or runs amok in the market-place with a cutlass and charges into a brothel (*Abroad*), I understand what this quick little splinter of a man means to me, what the positive joy of his performances is all about: Hawtrey implies the possibility of happiness.

1. A Cock in a Frock I
Hawtrey as Charlotte Tree in
Counterfeit! at the Duke of York's
Theatre (1939).

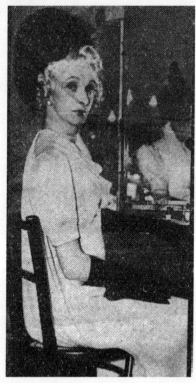

2. **A Cock in a Frock II**
Hawtrey as Natasha (with John
Bentley as Helmuth) in the
Ruritanian sketch 'Under
Which Flag' in the revue *New
Faces*, at the Comedy Theatre
(1940).

3. Feliks Topolski's
drawing of Hawtrey
as the Vivandière
in the revue *New
Faces*.

4. A Cock in a Frock III
Hawtrey as Madame René in the revue *Scoop!* at the Vaudeville
Theatre (1942).

5. What a Whopper!
Hawtrey with Kenneth Williams in *Carry On Constable* (1959).

6. 'Oh! Hello!'
Hawtrey in *Carry On Cleo* (1964).

Entr'acte

. . .

I do not see any chance of having anything to offer you in the immediate future.
24 May 1939

I regret that I have nothing at the moment.
9 October 1946

Of course I know your work and shall certainly remember you when casting future programmes.
21 October 1946

Of course I will remember you if anything comes along.
7 November 1946

I won't forget that you would like to do some broadcasting if a suitable part should crop up.
27 June 1947

I have nothing quite in your line at the moment.
21 January 1948

I won't forget you as soon as something you would like comes along.
1 June 1948

You can be assured that should there be any part that seems to me to respond to your particular gifts, I shall not forget you.
25 June 1948

I am sorry to hear Variety Producers have not been in touch.
2 December 1954

I am afraid I cannot be of any immediate assistance.
24 December 1954

I am sorry that nothing else has turned up for you for quite a time, but you are on my list and perhaps one day . . .
4 January 1955

I am afraid I have nothing at all to offer you at the moment.
5 January 1955

Of course I won't forget you if anything remotely suitable crops up.
14 January 1955

Mr Amyes regrets that for the moment he is unable to arrange any interviews.
20 January 1955

Unfortunately Miss Allen has very little production work in hand at present.
3 February 1955

I am afraid I will not be casting for months and months.
21 February 1955

Mr H. B. Fortnin would be very pleased to see you, though he doesn't think he will have a chance to offer you a part in the near future.
10 March 1955

I am quite sure Mr Leonard Brett will remember you when casting in the future.
4 April 1955

I am afraid I cannot be at all helpful at the moment as I am at present responsible for only a small number of productions each year and I do not expect to be casting again for some time.
17 February 1956

I will most certainly keep you in mind for my future programme.
20 February 1956

Mr Clayton has asked me to write and thank you for your letter [. . .] I am afraid that his next play has already been cast [. . .] I am sorry about this, but there it is.
5 March 1956

Unfortunately I have nothing suitable to offer you at the moment.
13 March 1956

The producer has noted your name on his casting list and will bear you in mind should there be any suitable part in a future production.
23 March 1956

. . .

7. 'Come on and give it to me, big boy!'
Hawtrey as Private Widdle in *Carry On Up the Khyber* (1968).

8. Private Widdle *en travesti*.

9. Hawtrey as the world's least reassuring gynaecologist.

10. **A Cock in a Frock IV** Hawtrey in his element as Lady Puddleton in *Carry On Again Doctor* (1969).

11. Hawtrey as the world's least reassuring psychotherapist.

12. 'Hello Sailor – show us your growler!'
Hawtrey in a leisure moment (Brighton, 1971).

13. **A Burnt Out Case**
Hawtrey after the fire (1984).

14. **The Helmet's Last Stand.**

PART TWO

Life

After such comprehensive rejection, no wonder Hawtrey turned to drink. His many letters, appealing for work, angling for advancement, are literally pathetic [*pathetikos*: exciting pity or sadness]: 'I was talking to a mutual friend today – Lady Ulick Browne – Elma – and she was horrified to learn that I didn't televise more frequently, and she advised me to contact you at Lime Grove. I telephoned your office this morning, but you were attending a meeting,' he wrote to a Mr Norman Rutherford in 1955. 'I am now free,' he'd tell all manner of producer and impresario. 'I should be very grateful if you would kindly keep me in mind, and look forward to an opportunity of working for you' . . . 'I very much regret not having worked for you for so long, and should be very grateful if you would kindly keep me in mind' . . . 'I think you will agree there would be room for my services if my availability were known' . . . 'I need hardly say that my face is no longer new but rather old and familiar' . . .; and it is almost heartbreaking to hear him entreat: 'Please don't forget me.'*

* Hawtrey's begging letters must have been received by everybody at Broadcasting House, from the Director-General to the janitors. Recipients included: Brandon Acton Ward, Douglas Allen, Mary Allen, Julian Amyes, Ian Atkins, T. Holland Bennett, Alan Bromley, Harry Caldwell, Kenneth Cartier, Rudolph Cartier, Harold Clayton, Douglas Cleverdon, Cleland Finn, Vernon Harris, Campbell Logan, Robert MacDermot, Cecil McGivern, Graeme Muir, Harry S. Pepper, Raymond Raikes, Shaun Sutton, Robert Tronson, Bill Ward, etc., all radio or television apparatchiks, and not a single one of these names rings any bells with me.

The Man who was Private Widdle

It was as if he were a translucent phantom, weightless, a nothingness. His agents, Al Parker Ltd, didn't fare much better on his behalf ('Our client is very anxious to do some broadcasting,' they stated in 1948 to Bill Ward at Alexandra Palace); and in September 1952, Hawtrey wrote to Gordon Smith, the Drama Booking Manager, from the Royal Turks Head Hotel, Newcastle upon Tyne, where he was touring in a French farce, *Husbands Don't Count*, to remind the BBC all over again who he was:

> I first broadcast in 1939, and have worked for all
> departments of Drama and Variety since that time,
> though in recent years I have been mainly occupied with
> Films and Theatre.

Films were, of course, the Will Hay puerilities, except his death in 1948 put paid to those, and walk-ons in pre-*Carry On* items by Peter Rogers; in *To Dorothy a Son* he has to deliver a tongue-twister ('Bloke's back brakelight's broke'*) and in *Please Turn Over* he was a jeweller or pawnbroker. He also worked for Ealing Studios, under Michael Balcon. 'In the film *Passport to Pimlico* I composed the music, and played it in the picture,' he alleged – not wholly truthfully, as the score was by Georges Auric, who had collaborated with Cocteau since before the 1920s and who became director of the Paris Opéra. What Hawtrey does do, in this great movie, is play a piano in a scene set in the pub, the Duke of Burgundy. He's Bert Fitch, the potboy, collecting glasses,

---

* That's what Peter Rogers himself told me. I have now, however, seen this film, screened on a wet afternoon by Channel Four, and the actual line is 'back brake block's broke' – and it is spoken by Mona Washbourne's District Nurse, not by Hawtrey, who plays the porter at a hotel, carrying Shelley Winters' monogrammed luggage. He looks like an ephebe – a foetus; and how could anybody, even after fifty years, confuse Charles Hawtrey and Mona Washbourne?

carrying trays upstairs, and at one point he jostles through the crowd, sits at the joanna and plonks out a tune. It's a sort of vamp-till-ready series of arpeggios; lots of tinkling scales and chords.*

In the film, Pimlico is a bit of London which becomes as exotic as abroad. (It is unseasonably hot and pavement cafés and ceiling fans add to the Mediterranean mood.) Old documents, discovered in a hidden vault opened by a bomb blast, prove that the district isn't English; it's rightfully an outpost of a French dukedom, so the inhabitants declare themselves independent – with the classic line, 'We always were English, and we always will be English, and it's just because we're English we're sticking out for our rights to be Burgundians!' *Passport to Pimlico* succeeds on all sorts of levels. It is a British dream of liberation, from interfering officials and the wartime rationing of foodstuffs and luxuries; it is a veritable documentary of 1940s life, the bombsites, clothing coupons, trains and streetscapes. (It records a lost London.) It is also a masterpiece of ensemble acting – Stanley Holloway, Margaret Rutherford, Raymond Huntley, Basil Radford and Naunton Wayne. In my mind's eye, the past is wholly populated by such characters, riding by on their bicycles, doffing their bowlers, furling their umbrellas. If the *Carry On* team were knock-about over-age children out on a spree, the Ealing actors are a dream of what adults ought to be like: nice uncles, dotty maiden aunts, kindly parents, nosey but good-hearted neighbours; a community

---

* Jonathan Coe writes: 'I find it utterly fascinating that Hawtrey should have claimed to have *written the music* for *Passport to Pimlico* on the basis that he plays the piano in one scene! This is somehow far more disturbing and delusional than lying about his parentage. What a very, very strange little man he was.' (Letter to author, 27 November 2000. Fact: before he became a distinguished novelist Jonathan Coe used to play the piano in a lesbian pub called The Purple Passage in Welwyn Garden City.)

of improbable goodness and refinement. The decency, of course, is as artificial as the pantomimic poster-paint of the *Carry On*s, so how does Hawtrey fit in? During shooting, in July 1948, he enjoyed playing poker, in a hut built on the set in Lambeth, with Hermione Baddeley, Stanley Holloway and Betty Warren. He's sunny and feckless, and yet his Bert Fitch is on the brink of gormlessness. Without the ponderous and pompous Will Hay to play off against – as, later, he'd play off his own brand of camp against the distortions of Kenneth Williams – Hawtrey has no particular flavour. He's like his piano-playing, a bit wishy-washy.

His theatre appearances, too, at this juncture, suggest a round of operetta and other vapidities. I have found a long-playing microgroove, *Songs of Stage and Screen* (Parlophone – Odeon), recorded some time in the 1940s, and Hawtrey, pictured on the sleeve in Mozart-era costume, is to be heard accompanying Richard Tauber in numbers from Walter Ellis's *Old Chelsea* and Sir Edward German's *Merrie England*. 'Certain it is that this record will bring memories flooding back into the mind,' says the jacket note, archly, 'memories of colourful shows . . . and of people once we knew.' Hawtrey had been Peter Crawley, when *Old Chelsea* ('A New Musical Romance'*) had opened at the Princes Theatre in February 1943. His duets with Betty Percheron included 'When a Boy Meets a Girl', 'A Holiday for Chelsea' and 'When I Write Home about You'. Old

---

* 'The interludes of plot and rhymes
    Do not permit much space to give
  A faithful telling of the times
    And how our forebears used to live.
  So, asking pardon, scrutineers,
    With only songs and roundalays,
  We speak but vaguely of the years,
    And call it Chelsea's olden days.' *Christ!*

64

Chelsea, in fact, was pretty much like old Vienna; as *The Times* put it, 'for the customary lilac there is wisteria, but the sun is perpetually what the prima donna would call gladsome forsooth'. It sounds horrendously saccharine – the sub-Schubert music, the less than Léhar-esque mood; a 'honey-coloured, jasmine-scented jamboree', in the words of a contemporary critic. 'Miss Betty Percheron and Mr Charles Hawtrey are doomed to a childishness which is intended to be gracefully child-like.'

The episode suggests what was going wrong with Hawtrey's career. He'd prolonged being a child actor or juvenile player for as long as possible (he was thirty-one when appearing with Hay in variety at the Victoria Palace after the war); the freakshow of the *Carry On*s was well into the future (it could be argued that the *Carry On*s were for people who generally couldn't be employed elsewhere – nancys, hysterics, grotesques); intimate revue and cabaret, where he bloomed, was a fading form. He was too peculiar for people to know what to do with. (Into what is precociousness meant to evolve?) Of his Walter Wilkins, in *Merrie England*, at the Winter Garden Theatre, Drury Lane, in October 1944, for example, it was said, 'Charles Hawtrey's is a witty and elegant performance, though on a rather miniature scale.'

He'd get better as he got older, as the urchin in him refused to lie low. But in this period of his protracted adolescence or unnaturally deferred puberty, he seemed simply fey, a bright speck, like a humming bird. All he appeared cut out for was light musical comedy. 'I would like to point out that I am a musical artiste,' he told the BBC. His agent backed him up. 'Although this artiste is well-known for his work in straight plays and musical productions, he has a "songs at the piano" act, which he is very keen to televise.' Eventually, Hawtrey coerced the Corporation into giving him an audition. He wrote to Pat Newman, in May 1950:

> I have had much experience in Cabaret in which I sing amusing and popular songs at a piano, and I propose doing this for you, that is, if you will kindly grant me an audition.

The opportunity to shine was given to him four months later, on 25 September. That Hawtrey kept up his barrage of chirpy, chippy letters long afterwards suggests he didn't know what a disaster he was, how damningly he'd been received. Here are the notes written on the spot:

> Does not make the grade as a songs-at-the-piano merchant. Old-fashioned material sung straight but no good nowadays.

> Sang a song he called the 'Passing Twenties' but he should have burlesqued the period and not sung the song straight. His 'straight' song was sung in the same vein. He should stick to his acting. No use to us.

> Oh, Charles, No. Let us draw a decent veil across this. Stick to acting.

> A pleasant little party act, but not suitable for featuring on radio, rather a dated style.

Hawtrey evidently didn't do justice to himself. He made the mistake of trying to ingratiate by being thin and brittle – instead of coming on in full drag, a strange fruit – and an over-ripe one at that. He was graded '5 minus', literally abysmal, and in the light of these remarks,* Geoffrey E. O. Riggs' letter, sent to Hawtrey on 29 September, is impressive

---

* His examiners were Joan Clark, Freddie Piffard, A. Scott-Johnson and Charles Maxwell. On the off-chance that you know them or any of their immediate descendants, a Brock's banger through the letterbox please.

in its ambiguity; he implies the slightest degree of hope when, of course, as we now know, none whatever existed. (As Doctor Johnson would say, Hawtrey was fed with a 'continual renovation of hope, to end in a constant succession of disappointment'):

Dear Mr Hawtrey,

Thank you for attending the audition on Monday 25th September 1950, as the result of which we now have full details of the nature and standard of your performance.

You will, no doubt, appreciate that the selection of artists from the large number suitable for broadcasting is governed by our programme requirements. If, however, an opportunity should occur to offer you an engagement in Variety programmes broadcast from our London Studios, we will, of course, communicate with you again.

Yours faithfully

. . .

Does not make the grade . . . *No use to us* . . . *Oh, Charles, No* . . . *not suitable* . . . Four years later (see Appendix), he was still puzzled as to why he couldn't get many assignments outside of the Children's Hour remit, which he found stifling; and at one point he wondered whether the thing to do was become a producer. 'Are you interested in Charles Hawtrey as a producer?' a BBC internal memo asked incredulously. 'Training School?' On the thin scrap of paper departmental heads have scribbled in ink:

Just a 'possible' for Light Entertainment [television] but I'm not violently keen.

Hawtrey ranks far down on the list of applicants that Drama must at present refuse.

The Man who was Private Widdle

This time the rejection letter (from 'Controller Programmes') was more robust: 'I am afraid I must tell you that we can see little opportunity of using your services.' Neither radio nor television was keen to accommodate him.

What was the problem? What was it the BBC couldn't see or were put off by? The campery, which he was trying to sweeten by immersing himself in Ivor Novello, Sigmund Romberg and operetta, but which was really suggestive of absinthe drinkers and outrageousness? His individuality, which gave his performances an air of day-dreaminess – yet paradoxically he's always conscious of an audience, of playing to people? Perhaps there was only room for one licensed queer, and that was Frankie Howerd, heavy-set and doleful, shooting appalled glances at all the old ladies in his audience who insisted on detecting innuendos in his patter ('Eh? Oooerr, missus!'), scowling, beaming, lip-smacking, rambling, and full of sauce. But with Howerd it *was* innuendo. Hawtrey was more forthright, and yet his proclivities were wholly illegal until the Sexual Offences Act of 1967; asked to put his arms around Barbara Windsor for the cameras at a press reception, he ran from the room crying, 'No, thank you. Find me a gentleman instead!' On another occasion, up in Manchester on a publicity tour, he chased Barbara Windsor and George Best with a plastic axe. 'There were 2,000 girls, and Charlie, all screaming for Georgie,' Miss Windsor tells me. 'Charlie went off into the night with a little smile on his face.' For surely in the whole of Lancashire there'd be some chap he could flood with love's effusion? Hawtrey, it could be said, was in the wrong era. Everything has to be camp now, from Eddie Izzard to Graham Norton,* from Dale

* What a long way we've travelled. Norton, an irritatingly cheerful leprechaun who'd be Life President of the Friends of Charlie, should such a brotherhood exist, and whose show *So Graham Norton* treats us to conversations with

Winton to Matthew Kelly to Ainsley Harriott washing a cucumber. The surest means of getting your own television show is to be what Wilde called an Uranian. Half a century ago, however, the only way Hawtrey could get work of any kind was to offer to take a twenty-five per cent cut in the standard rate of pay. Josephine Burton, on behalf of Al Parker Ltd, wrote to David Manderson of the BBC on 15 June 1948 to confirm that 'our client is prepared to reduce his basic fee over a trial period, as you suggested, to see whether the extra work that will come to him will recompense him for this'. She added, 'It is, of course, to be clearly understood that our client's agreement to meet you regarding terms will in no way prejudice his professional status . . . after all, he has been broadcasting steadily since 1929, and has always been happy to co-operate in any way.'

Not unexpectedly, Hawtrey's gesture or gambit failed. When the self-imposed six-month period expired, he let another half year go by, and then told Burton in July 1949 that 'I have, in fact, Broadcast less than at any time, notwithstanding the Booking Department's knowledge of my availability.' Informed of this, the BBC of course denied all knowledge of any agreement, formal or implied. If Hawtrey had wanted less money, that was his affair; a flood of extra work would never have been promised or guaranteed. 'I hardly think I should be foolish enough to have given any artist an assurance that, on the reduction of their fee by twenty-five per-cent, a greater number of engagements would necessarily follow than had been the case over a

---

punters on a German telephone sex line and a woman on the internet playing 'Voodoo Lady' with a penny whistle stuck up her maiden-trap, has said that homosexuals are so happy and acceptable these days, there is no need to worry you'll end up a sad loner 'walking your dog on a beach in Deal' – precisely Hawtrey's pathetic fate, except he didn't have a dog (*Radio Times*, 28 October–3 November 2000).

specified period in the past,' thundered Manderson, adding, 'I fail to understand why Hawtrey is grumbling . . .'

Hawtrey would receive ten guineas; occasionally fifteen or twenty, if rehearsals were involved. Of necessity he was frugal, penny-pinching. He maintained his account at the Royal Bank of Scotland (Piccadilly branch), because he believed the Scots would keep a beadier eye on their customers' shillings. He'd lug bags of carrots from Leeds to Kent, because vegetables were cheaper in Yorkshire. He pilfered toilet rolls from public lavatories – or at least his mother did. She was notorious for wiping out supplies at Pinewood and, when rumbled, tried to flush away the incriminating evidence, which blocked the drains, closing down production on *Chitty Chitty Bang Bang*. Hawtrey was told that in future his mother would have to be locked in his dressing room. At Pinewood he avoided the restaurant, where a table was reserved for the *Carry On* team, and ate alone in the canteen, with the lower-echelon crew and cleaning staff. In London, his idea of a treat was not the Dorchester but the café in Bourne & Hollingsworth, the department store, or Marshall & Snelgrove, Oxford Street, with its Corset Salon on the first floor. Except when he retired to Deal, and for a brief period in the late 1960s when he and his mother moved to 66 Mortlake Road, Kew, Surrey (telephone PRO 9139), he never left the odorous family home, 217 Cromwell Road, Hounslow, Middlesex (telephone HOU 8875). He chain-smoked Weights cigarettes, the cheapest brand on the market. He drank supermarket gin decanted into quart-sized R. White's lemonade bottles, which he shared with his cat. As Hattie Jacques said, 'What can you expect from someone who has a strange mother and an alcoholic cat?' The cat, pampered with port-soaked sugar lumps, its bread and butter sprinkled with Cyprus sherry, used to walk into doors and see double when chasing mice. Hawtrey had heated arguments with it, or pleasant conversations, long into the night. 'Wave, you cunt!' Hawtrey would implore, if the moggy fell silent or gave him the cold shoulder. He travelled by bus, or walked – hence astounding Laurence Olivier. (A man further off from the grandiosity of Larry and Viv's Notley Abbey it is scarcely possible to imagine.) What he was like to be with on a journey is illustrated by his sandwich-making routine in a second-class carriage on the Wolverhampton to Euston train, *circa* 1979. He's with another actor from a pantomime, Bryan Johnson, who states that he wasn't happy travelling with Hawtrey as 'he always got pretty emotional if anyone recognized him, so I armed myself with a lot of newspapers to hide behind should the occasion arise. Charlie asked if I'd like a sandwich, pushed his glasses to the top of his head and disappeared into his duffle bag. Out came a loaf of white sliced bread, a packet of butter, a lump of cheese, and a plastic knife. He did everything so slowly, examining each item very, very closely, as if he was thinking, "So, this is cheese, eh?" Well of course, as the train filled up, people realized that here was Charles Hawtrey, cutting sandwiches. He appeared not to notice the crowd that was gathering. The butter wouldn't spread; the bread disintegrated. "You great huge buxom boy, would you prefer ham or cheese?" he asked. Then his plastic knife broke. I was exhausted watching him and watching the passengers watching him. "Would you like another one, dear boy?"'

What a woeful picnic. His dingy quality is there in abundance. But if they weren't going to pay him handsomely, at least he could be inched up the billing roster and have his name printed in block capitals or placed above the title.

Again this ambition was frequently thwarted and he'd make a huge fuss. Like Andrew Aguecheek, he acquired a reputation for being 'a great quarreler'. It grieved him that he'd been gainfully employed as an actor since he was scarcely out of nappies, and yet he hadn't really got anywhere in terms of status and glory. His stars shone darkly over him; and on the subject of stardom, as far back as 1948 he was agitating for recognition. Here's a letter from a John Glyn-Jones:

I have been into the question of possible star billing for *Chain Male* [*sic*] and am very sorry to say that I don't see how it can be managed. I don't want to give any star billings for this show and if I had to do so it would obviously be very invidious to single out your part from others of equal size on the grounds that it is being played by an artist of your experience. I am sure this will not comfort you much, but I hope that on reflection you will see that were we to do as you ask it would involve us in a never-ending series of requests from artists in a similar position to yourself.

In other words, as they'd say in Michigan, fuck you and the horse you rode in on. The scenario repeated itself in September 1960, when Hawtrey decided he no longer wanted to be billed equally with Patricia Hayes for *Norman and Henry Bones*:

I have had a long talk today with Mr Hawtrey [wrote Terry Carney, of Eric L'Epine Smith Ltd, his new agent], and he still disagrees with the billing 'and Patricia Hayes' [. . .] Charles feels that at this stage of his career [. . .] he would wish the billing to be –

Life

CHARLES HAWTREY
With
PATRICIA HAYES*

He, therefore, feels that if this could not be agreed to
then you would possibly be able to recast the part with
perhaps a younger artist [. . .] *I can assure you that
Mr Hawtrey is adamant on this point* [my italics].

What Patricia Hayes may have thought about her suggested demotion is not recorded, but Hawtrey worked with
her son, Richard O'Callaghan, in *Loving*, and had a crush
on him. So keen was Hawtrey to see the fresh-faced actor
shoot the scenes with Imogen Hassall and Jacki Piper that
he'd rush back from his dressing room in his half-hose, his
face still covered with pink make-up and blobs of cotton
wool.

His bluff was duly called where billing (and I assume cooing) was concerned. 'We regret that we are unable to accept
Charles Hawtrey's proposed billing, so if he still feels that he
must withdraw from the cast of *Norman and Henry Bones*
on that account then we shall be very sorry to lose his services,' L'Epine Smith were told. The point of pride or prin-
ciple lost him thirty guineas a week, and earned him the label
of intractable. Hawtrey's association with the *Carry Ons*
foundered in a similar fashion. Lance Percival took over his
role as the seasick ship's cook in *Cruising* because there was
a disagreement over 'all major paid advertizing' (i.e. where
his name would go on the poster); and Hawtrey refused to
appear in Thames Television's 1972 edition of *Carry On*

---

* Or what he'd really want if he were honest:

CHARLES HAWTREY
(with Patricia Hayes)

73

*Christmas** because he was insulted to be billed beneath Hattie Jacques, all nineteen stone seven pounds of her.

According to Barbara Windsor, 'There was no such thing as billing really, it depended on what you were doing. Charlie let Gerald Thomas down badly just two days before filming and so he was never used again, which was a great shame as he was my favourite actor in the team.' Actually, billing did matter to the producers, otherwise why didn't they cave in instantly to what might seem an actor's mere caprices? Rogers and Thomas wanted Hattie Jacques' name first to capitalize on her television pre-eminence, in the sitcom with Eric Sykes. They knew what they were about. Hawtrey would have been further incensed, however, had he ever known about the confidential Rank Organisation House Note, dated 25 May 1972, that's to say around six months earlier, where Lloyd's, the insurers, informed the studio that owing to Hattie Jacques' ballooning weight and blood pressure problems, 'no cover whatsoever can be given in respect [of her] for any future film'. She shouldn't have been allowed to work, unless for telly you can be less cautious? *Carry On Christmas* was made of course for Thames, and was therefore outside of Rank's jurisdiction.

Gerald Thomas had done his best to discuss matters with the actor but Hawtrey went to ground. Then he remembered to phone the department stores, Dickins & Jones and Swan & Edgar . . . 'I found him having lunch at Bourne & Hollingsworth and . . . tried to talk him into changing his mind. In

---

* Robert Ross, in *The Carry On Companion*, explains the background to the sorry saga. A *Carry On Christmas* television special had been produced in 1969 and 1970. In 1971, the first show was repeated, and in December 1972, because Sid James, Kenneth Williams and Terry Scott were not to be involved, Hawtrey demanded top billing, not unreasonably. In the latest film, *Abroad*, Hawtrey was third on the list, while Hattie Jacques was way down the roster in eleventh place, next to June Whitfield.

on't you piss off? You're always trying to be so nice
one.' Fellow artistes dreaded sharing digs with him
he pantomime season. He'd shout and bawl on the
generally create, and Kenneth Williams told his
s not the eccentricity, or the grotesquerie, or the
ality that puts one off Charles: it is the excruciat-
m.' There again, perhaps Williams was jealous.
llow legs himself and tended to show off when
Hawtrey was he like Caliban seeing his own
e in the looking-glass? In real life both men
dly spirit and suffered cold, neglected lives.
a writer or painter in the grip of the grog,
to see your grief and disappointment; you can
reak. But if you are an actor? And an actor of
, drawn to velveteen and lace, face-paints
ith him the stage, the world of the theatre,
credibly beautiful things – Vivien Leigh,
rocks, Tauber's tenor – and I think he didn't
k to reality after that; he was always going
ddy, for its blur, its fuzziness, for the state
oblivion it can create. With Hawtrey,
lcohol abuse; it was a love affair. It was
avaged, pickled, tremulous, he was so
e, dipsomania became part of the per-
him in *Cowboy*, sucking at a whisky
asses in the saloon, taking sly slugs of
leap, the Indian Chief, he is at his most
he collapses in the gaol and has to be
by a pair of ranchers. How hard did
thirst built into his character or were
s on the set?
awtrey was 'drinking in the morn-
work after more drinking during

the end I said, "Well, this is it. You have to make up your
mind finally right now, before you hang up. Will you accept
second billing or won't you?" There was a pause at the other
end of the line. Then he said, "No," and hung up.'

Hawtrey had burnt out his hopes. There was to be no
recognition of his long loyal service. Rogers, however, who
had not even allowed the actor the harmless vanity of a small
silver cardboard star for his dressing-room door, was
unforgiving. 'There was no question that Charles Hawtrey
was going to hold me to ransom – no way that we'd trust
Charles Hawtrey after letting us down like that, so we never
used him again.'

He really can't see why the actor should regard himself a
victim; and when they were making *Don't Lose Your Head*,
the one about the French Revolution, the wonder is that
the cast didn't grab their chance to shove Rogers under the
guillotine. The gulf between how he and his wife Betty Box
lived – Aston Martins, Rolls Royces ('I had two at a time. A
saloon and a convertible'), floor-length mink coats and
chauffeur-driven trips to the Royal Ballet ('the barman
became a personal friend and would always have champagne and a tray of smoked salmon sandwiches ready during
the interval') – and how the actors lived (Kenneth Williams
and Hawtrey eating out of tins in shabby bedsits) is as
laughably wide as that which divided the court of Louis XVI
from the horny-handed peasantry.

Rogers would smile wanly at such a comparison and has
anyway heard it all before. Hawtrey, for instance, accused
him of being drunk with power – to which Rogers retorted
that *he* wasn't the one who was drunk, which is chillingly
true. Rogers was always sober-sided to a fault; niggardly, in
fact. 'I do my best to make a film on time and under budget,
that's all,' he has said flatly. If he treated his subordinates (or

assets) abruptly or less than compassionately, well, you can't expect a generalissimo's authority to be questioned. The *Carry On*s, two or three fully fledged pictures a year, had to be completed with severe military precision. 'I make a film in five working weeks and it makes a fortune,' he explained.

It's not that he didn't want to dish the gravy around or that the actors had a horrible time, standing about in the rain or being ticked off if they needed a second take; it's the long-term effects of what being cut down to size generally had on Hawtrey that's my present concern. Feeling himself to be unappreciated and ignored, he forced a lonely and bleak existence upon himself; as did Kenneth Williams, too, who was similarly filled with a sense of failure and disgust. Where Williams lived sequestered with his mother in a pristine flat, the sparkling toilet out of bounds to visitors, the stove wrapped in cellophane, a manically antiseptic environment that reflected his abhorrence of contact, with other people, with germs, with the give and take of life itself ('the sharing of a life is what makes a life,' he said, 'and I cannot share because I dare not risk the vulnerability involved'), Hawtrey lived, also with his mother, amongst the dust and clutter of the Edwardian era: fans, watercolours, china, silk screens, a piano flanked by brass candelabra, palm leaves, cases of stuffed birds, and the fumes of oil lamps and sickly-sweet face powder and colognes. Williams inhabited a spotless mortuary, Hawtrey went home to a cobwebby mausoleum; and they were both lurid real-life Mr Bleaneys, the ultimate sad loner invented by Philip Larkin, full of melancholy, sitting 'through days of thin continuous dreaming'.

'Charles is a bit of a lonely man,' said Thomas after his final phone call with the actor. 'So more than any other member of the team, he used to volunteer to go to various cinemas all over the country to help promote one of the

films. Of course he would be win[...] big fuss of and all I can think is[...] sense of his own importance.' W[...] to scream along with the fans f[...]

This reasoning seems a bit [...] By accusing Hawtrey of irrit[...] saying that his judgement [...] poorly controlled, Thoma[...] showed symptoms of d[...] think Hawtrey's obsessi[...] or his making a show [...] prestige, in the end. [...] producers were doin[...] he was dependent[...] him, knocking hir[...] his huge hunger f[...] desolate. As he [...] ing of *Jungle*, i[...] traitors, but s[...] but of cours[...]

He had [...] superstar[...] develope[...] alleviat[...] the dri[...] tippli[...] whis[...] and [...] pr[...]

'Why [...] to every[...] during t[...] stairs an[...] diary: 'It[...] homosexu[...] ing bored[...] He had ho[...] drunk. Wit[...] distorted fa[...] lacked a frie[...] If you are[...] nobody needs[...] conceal heartb[...] Hawtrey's kin[...] and filigree? W[...] was full of in[...] Beatrice Lillie's f[...] fancy coming bac[...] to be prone to a t[...] of exaltation or [...] though, it wasn't a[...] alcohol rapture. R[...] soaked in jungle ju[...] formance. Look at [...] flask, finishing off g[...] the firewater. As Big F[...] joyful, and eventually[...] carried out of the scen[...] he have to act? Was his[...] they utilizing how he w[...] Rogers recalls that H[...] ings, and half asleep fo[...]

lunch. He was holding up production' – and as nothing could be allowed to do that, if he passed out cold it was captured on camera. Before the stunt sequence in *Spying*, where he had to fall about on a conveyor belt, get hit by rocks and have his clothes ripped off, he fortified himself royally. For much of the scene, as edited, he's on his back. 'Have you tried giving him a nip of brandy?' asked the unit nurse, perturbed that Hawtrey hadn't come to after a take. 'That's the last thing he needs, dear!' said Kenneth Williams. 'The scene took an interminable time to get in the can,' Dilys Laye remembers, 'and Hawtrey wasn't a young man then, but he never complained, yet he was feeling quite queasy.' In *Doctor*, after his Mr Barron has attended the antenatal classes – this minuscule figure amidst the hippos – he is carried back whimpering to the ward by a couple of order-lies. Was he far gone and being propped up? (For the rest of the film he's in a bed, sleeping it off.)

At the conclusion of *Convenience*, when the annual works outing of W. C. Boggs & Son returns from the booze-up in Brighton, Hawtrey is to be seen curled up with the empties in the charabanc boot, snoozing. His Charles Coote is a favour-ite of mine. Plainly on the spirits, his demeanour is spiritual – the refined essence of camp. The way he enters the lounge room of his boarding-house, swerving through the door, squirming into his chair, flirting with the camera, blushing as Renée Houston, his landlady, confirms that 'I've put a new napkin in your ring': it is a dance worthy of Helpmann. Alcohol, at such moments, is transforming, transfigurative, as he totters and glides, leaps and lunges. (Didn't Chaplin have a drunk routine that was like ballet?) Drink, which was killing him, which was his all-consuming passion, was cap-able of creating the most sublime and prankish performances – and hence his swansong, *Abroad*, where he is gloriously delinquent. Here, as Eustace Tuttle, dipsomania *is* the character; he's always swigging from a bottle and swaying from side to side, and it is a gurgling, staggering (literally) accomplishment. He has a wonderful freedom, it seems to me; he's like a silent-movie actor, the way he looks and moves, appearing on the beach in diving goggles and knocking back his pot of suntan lotion. For some reason he appears in June Whitfield's bath, nonchalantly sipping a huge glass of plonk.

Joe McGrath told me that he saw Hawtrey at the Associated-Rediffusion studios during the making of the series *Our House* all the way back in 1960, busy swigging from a flask in the dressing room. 'He was outrageous,' says Joe. ' "Hello, darling!" ' Yet his performance never faltered once, and Norman Hudis recalls the beauty of some of Hawtrey's trance-like improvisations. 'There was a huge wall-safe behind his desk. "Pity to waste such a gorgeous prop," he said. We thought no more about it – but Charlie did. Before we went in front of the live audience, he asked the director, Ernest Maxin, to stay on him at the end of the scene. Ernest did so – and Charlie opened the safe and took out a brown paper bag – emptied it – it contained his lunch. Huge laugh. Another time, we were running a few minutes short so I threw together a mime sequence for Charlie – packing his things and making a slapstick hash of it. Though he tottered through it perfectly, he rather spoilt the effect by muttering and mumbling to himself . . .'

Yet the effrontery of his art was less amusing in life. His socializing skills went and he ceased to care. Fatigue and depression overtook him. What we are watching, in these tanked up performances, is a mind on the slide. As Peter Rogers told me, 'If Hawtrey had a boyfriend on the go, he'd be fine. Charming, erudite. If he was feeling lonely or rejected, he'd go to pieces – a complete change of personality. He'd be continually drunk and we'd have to force black coffee down him – stand him up and support him between two people. Appalling. But on the whole – yes, very lonely.'

Not that Hawtrey minded being manhandled. One November, on his birthday, the crew planned to give him the bumps. (He was always ogling the grips and chippies and buying bars of chocolate for the props men: 'Does this thing really stretch human limbs?' he asked one of the crew, of the rack in *Henry*. 'Come into my room afterwards – and bring your smallest rack.') He fled – to be pursued and grappled by a stagehand, who lifted him up into his arms. Hawtrey let out a cry – a shout – all too literally an ejaculation. He'd been so excited and overcome that he had, so to speak, popped his light bulb, had an orgasm in his trousers. He slunk back to his dressing room flushed and shamefaced.

Hawtrey and sex is a sordid subject. (Asked if he'd been with a girl, he said he was sure it could be nice, but 'not as good as the real thing'.) He liked working-class lads in their teens, rent boys, off-duty merchant seamen and anybody connected with the Royal Marines School of Music, which had been founded in Deal in 1794. Unfortunately, far from being able to fellate buglers, all his pick-ups wanted to talk about was the *Carry On*s, which after the Hattie Jacques débâcle of 1972 and all that it summarized about the management of his career, he looked back on with loathing. 'The only reason I did them was that I needed regular money, like all actors. But after I had done seven or eight I realized I was typecast for ever and would never get proper work because of these films . . . They used me and dumped me.' He became foul-mouthed and violent, which is bleakly comical in itself when you think how dainty he was. 'Would you like to spit on my love-clump?' he'd ask. 'Would you like to grease my arse pipe? Let me consume your cock-broth?' It was fatal to ask for his autograph. Alan James Watson, who was nine in 1987, remembers seeing Hawtrey wearing a fur coat and a wide-brimmed hat in the middle of summer. 'Piss off!' the apparition said when approached. His normal greeting to inquisitive adults was a rounded 'Fuck off!', which could precipitate a punch-up, especially if a woman had tried to be familiar with him and her husband was nearby, overhearing Hawtrey's haughty dismissal. 'He did like Deal – particularly living so close to the sea,' recalls his neighbour, Joy Leonard, 'but he hated to be recognized.' A retired security man from Bourne & Hollingsworth, who lived in Deal, commented, 'Hawtrey's always pissed. Several of the pubs barred him. He can get very nasty you know'; and a local publican added, 'Millions of people think of him as a lovely person who makes them laugh. I try to remember him like that but I mostly think of him lying on my bar floor with his legs in the air absolutely plastered and incapable of speech.' Licensed premises where he'd used up his credit included The Carrier's Arms, St Margarets, and The Railway, Walmer, where he was slung out for screaming 'Landlord, my champagne is not chilled enough!' But he got banished from all the pubs in the area, one by one.

In 1980, eight years after Hawtrey had effectively disappeared from view, Patrick Newley, on behalf of the publisher William Kimber, attempted to track him down and see if he'd write his autobiography. Hawtrey was discovered in the Rockingham Club, Covent Garden, a dive frequented by drunks and drag queens. 'Most of the evening he was trying to pick up the rent boys,' recalls Newley, 'all of whom were more interested in asking him questions about Sid James, Kenneth Williams and Barbara Windsor. Charlie was furious.' Nothing came of the memoirs project ('Charlie wouldn't do anything and was pissed most of the time, so we never got anywhere');

but Newley saw enough of the actor to realize that 'he could be very funny and great company for a while and genuinely interesting to talk with, but then there were great depths of despair and hatred, black moods and, at times, paranoia.'

Tennessee Williams, catching sight of the elderly Garbo trudging along 35th Street like a bag lady, thought that she'd become 'the saddest of creatures, an artist who abandoned her art. That's worse than death.' Until his death in a Walmer hospital on 27 October 1988, this was exactly Hawtrey's ghost life, too. His appearances in pantomime, such as *Dick Whittington* at the Romiley Forum, *Snow White* in Telford, or *Mother Goose* in Preston, were so dishevelled and incoherent that the audiences lost patience and started talking amongst themselves. He turned down the role of Sir Henry Baskerville (played in the event by Kenneth Williams) in Peter Cook and Dudley Moore's ill-fated Holmes and Watson spoof. The other day I saw the film version of *Up Pompeii* (1971) and I wrote to Ned Sherrin, its producer, as follows:

> I much enjoyed *Up Pompeii* on the box; far less terrible than all the Guide Books would lead one to believe. I think it's perhaps that Frankie Howerd gets funnier, and our nostalgia for those old British comics (and comedies) intensifies over time. Now then, however, why didn't you think of using Charles Hawtrey, he really was something of a quirky genius . . .

For the film ('based on an idea by Talbot Rothwell') manages to find room for Bernard Bresslaw as Gorgo the Invincible, Nero's wrestling champion, grimacing and grinning in a Brian Blessed beard; as Frankie says, 'You nearly frightened me out of a year's growth.' And the innuendo-crammed script ('Honestly, you have to watch every word you say around here'), whilst naughtier, braver, than the *Carry Ons*, is, as Sotheby's would say, clearly school-of, circle-of and follower-of. Sherrin's reply, though, rather encapsulates why Hawtrey felt defeated, humiliated. 'Dear Roger, I think we kept off Charlie because he was *TOO* much a *Carry On* man ...' Yet *Up Pompeii*, with Bresslaw's and Rothwell's involvement, with Frankie's (Francis Bigger in *Doctor*, Professor Inigo Tinkle in *Up the Jungle*): it's a *Carry On* in all but name. Yet there we have it – Hawtrey was made to suffer the mortification and indignity of other people's ideas about his limitations and image, like Aguecheek who is written off as a fool.

He retreated to 117 Middle Street, Deal (telephone number 4686) and slammed the door behind him – and not only in a metaphorical sense. The few visitors allowed in had to make a roundabout route through the garage and the cellar, where he kept his train set. Kenneth Williams recalled seeing an unshaven, half-dressed Hawtrey appearing at a window. When he eventually found his way inside, after much ringing of the bell and shouting, Williams must have wished he hadn't bothered. The place was 'like a lodging house which all the boarders had suddenly deserted and that revolting smell of rising damp and cat's fish everywhere ...'* All Hawtrey wanted to do was show off his collection of male bongo magazines, *Whopper*, *Zipper*, *Campus Glory Holes* and *Touched by an Uncle*.

---

* At the time of writing (Autumn 2000), this Grade II-listed town house in the conservation area of Deal is for sale, at a price of £215,000, through Abbey Direct. It sounds much nicer than the dump Williams describes. 'The well-maintained accommodation is arranged over four floors retaining much of its charm and nostalgia through traditional features including fireplaces and panelled doors.' There are three reception rooms, four bedrooms, gas c/h and a ftd/kit. On the wall outside is a blue plaque – top billing at last:

Life

The place caught fire in August 1984. He'd left a cigarette burning in the lounge and the sofa ignited. Hawtrey was upstairs in bed with a sixteen-year-old, Steve, who rode a moped, and who'd earlier on spurted over the soft furnishings. Suddenly they realized the room was filling with smoke. Hawtrey dashed into the garden, bollock-naked, and raised the alarm. He then went to the top storey of the house so that a fireman would have to come and rescue him and carry him down on a ladder. He insisted that it had to be the biggest fireman, too, doing the lifting: Barry Bullock, who retired from Kent Fire Brigade's Retained Service shortly afterwards. Realizing that the actor was (still) bollock-naked, the officer offered him his big yellow helmet to cover his modesty. Hawtrey put it straight on his head, as he couldn't bear to be seen without his wig. 'You're all right now,' said the fireman when they reached the ground. 'No, I'm not,' Hawtrey replied. 'My fags are upstairs by the bed, and my boyfriend is in it.' Back up the ladder they went. As the spokesman from the police station laconically put it, 'Hawtrey was naked but the young lad had his trousers on.'

CHARLES
HAWTREY
1914–1988
Film, Theatre, Radio
& Television Actor
Lived Here

The property has been the subject of a feature article in *The Times* (23 September 2000). John Naish, the reporter, chortled at the concept of double frontages, substantial elevations and original knockers. 'The prim frontage gives no clue to its capacious behind. Inside, [there] is a warren of tight passages, stairs that need careful mounting and odd little cupboards and nooks. Some might think it a little too nooky, but in Hawtrey's world you could, of course, never have too much nooky.' Evidently, the spirit of Talbot Rothwell lives on.

Hawtrey refused medical treatment for his burns ('I regard myself as self-healing,' he mysteriously claimed) and was distraught at the ignominious way he'd been sprung from his lair. It was in all the tabloids ('NAKED ORDEAL FOR CARRY ON STAR, 68' blazed the *Sun*). He became a target for local vandals and lager louts, who shouted abuse through his letter-box; so as not to venture out he'd despatch a taxi to do his shopping, which mainly consisted of bringing in supplies of cooking sherry ('It's real sherry. It's from Cyprus'). He'd also order a taxi if he had to make a foray himself, if only for a hundred yards. (Dogs barked at him if he halted by them.) Accounts would be settled by cheque. He'd write out a cheque for fifty pence if that was all a journey cost. Though he'd shout at them if they were a minute late, cab drivers became Hawtrey's sole confidants. 'I could have been as famous as Sid James,' he'd complain. 'What did he have that I didn't? *Carry On Up the Jungle* was shot in a fucking greenhouse with clips of charging elephants cut in afterwards. I was quite deliberately frozen out of the top roles. I could've played them but I never got the chance . . . I got bugger all and at the end was shat on very badly . . .' If Hawtrey was told that the public loved him, that he was a star, he'd snap, 'What do you know about it? It was not your career that was ruined.' It wasn't long before every cabriolet and hackney carriage in Kent swerved and accelerated to avoid him.

If, as he believed, and with good cause, moguls and impresarios had rejected him, he took the only revenge possible, which was to reject his own public. After 1972 he lost confidence in himself – he lost the point of himself. For sixteen years he confessed, 'Getting drunk and dusting are all I do now.' He seldom answered his mail. He never answered the phone. He became invisible. His reclusiveness reached a

stage where he pretended not to exist – that Charles
Hawtrey was some other being, absent and travelling
abroad. 'Mr Hawtrey is away. He won't be back for three
months,' he'd tell callers, putting on a funny voice. Bizarrely,
where, in his revue days, he'd pretended to be a woman and,
in *Counterfeit!*, he'd played a woman, now he thought he
was a woman called Alice Dunne. A year before he died he
was approached by Colin Bourner, who was researching the
background to the *Carry Ons* for a possible thesis. Here,
dated 11 September 1987, is what Bourner received by way
of reply (there is no salutation):

> Reference – your letter addressed to Mr Charles Hawtrey,
> regarding the suggested reference to Mr Hawtrey in your
> proposed 'Book', and possible publication of same,
> with a prior meeting with Mr Hawtrey.
>
> Mr Hawtrey *forbids any* reference to him in
> this proposed 'Book', and will *not* permit a
> prior meeting.
>
> Mr Hawtrey is not available, and his whereabouts
> strictly private.
>
> Yours truly
>
> *Alice Dunne*

I've seen enough of Hawtrey's handwriting to pronounce
this, the pen scratching and stabbing at the paper, as authentic. In his time he'd received thousands of rejections to his
well-meaning enquiries; now it was his turn to issue the
knock-backs. Alice was his mother's name. Where does the
Dunne come from? (Irene Dunne, who'd played Queen Victoria in *The Mudlark*? John Gregory Dunne?) We know that
he had an Anthony Perkins-in-*Psycho* thing going with his

mother because people who shared his accommodation, during the dilapidated days of *Dick Whittington* and *Mother Goose*, used to hear him in the next room talking to her – having arguments and conversations – and yet she'd been dead for years. He was so isolated from people, he believed that only by talking to himself could he find a person who'd listen. This trait began or was first witnessed during *Up the Khyber*, in April 1968. Roy Castle told Colin Bourner,* 'Charlie was a difficult and eccentric man. Sometimes he used to stand in a corner talking to himself. He owned a block of flats when we were filming; he lived in one of them. He had a tenant who had to be evicted. It caused him a lot of trouble and preyed on his mind so much that he'd sit in a corner practising his conversations with the absent tenant.'

The flats would have been the Mr Bleaney bedsits Hawtrey created out of 66 Mortlake Road, Kew, when his mother died. Neighbours grew to dread the commotion of taxis coming and going in the small hours. Doors slamming, dustbins falling over, cats screeching, dogs howling, milk bottles being smashed underfoot, sash-windows shooting up and women in curlers shoving their heads out and telling Hawtrey to pipe down.

'Gissa kiss, gissa kiss,' he'd be imploring.

'I'm not going to kiss you – I just want my fare,' the taxi driver would be saying with increasing exasperation.

'No kissy kissy, no fare.'

'I want my money.'

'I want to be kissed. Come here, whip out your love nub.'

'I'll call the police.'

It's a miracle he was never thumped half to death and

* Who kindly gave the notes for his aborted project to me.

dumped on the steps of a casualty department. He was particularly keen on burly black men.

At the same time as Castle beheld Hawtrey jabbering to himself, Kenneth Williams was recording in his diary 'the saga of Hawtrey moving into the one room at his house. It was unbelievably sordid' (5 April 1968). Why sordid? Because of the flowered curtains 'thin and frayed, fall[ing] to within five inches of the sill; the window show[ing] a strip of building land, tussocky, littered' (Larkin)? Because of the sheer non-glamour of Hawtrey's surroundings and how this contrasted with the beautiful inventions of his performances? Because the pad or gaff, where the off-stage, off-screen life gets lived, represented the black hole that's reality? Hawtrey himself had a less metaphysical object in view. He hoped to fill the property with grateful guests, transients and runaways, and with luck he'd awake each morning to find his flat full of sailors' empty cigarette packets.

It wasn't to be; all that happened was that he was ripped off. He'd still, however, pretend to people that he was leading a full life – what Williams called his 'irritating desire to score or be intriguing' – and instead of being able to go on holiday like anybody else, he'd have to insist that, as he did after *Again Doctor*, 'I'm taking a false beard and travelling under an assumed name, to allay suspicion'. Of what? That he was somebody else entirely? There wasn't much he could do with what John Updike, in an essay on the art of caricature, would call Hawtrey's 'widely recognised countenance'. Yet he was outraged (and outrageous) about what he saw as invasions of privacy, of propriety, and of style. He was convinced people were using him, and after his mother died his faith in everybody went. She'd been so devoted to him, such a smothering presence, that in her absence he felt diminished – just as he felt he was being diminished by his audiences and the BBC and the executives of Pinewood. He was afraid to venture far – indeed he couldn't venture far. Taxis declined to be hailed by him; pubs had barred him. He'd well and truly boxed himself in. 'Unfortunately he bleated and moaned so much that a lot of people who had sympathy for him got very tired of it and, at the end, he ran out of friends. He seemed to cut himself off deliberately and to enjoy doing so,' explained a neighbour.

Did he enjoy doing so, I wonder? There's certainly a neat symmetry about his life and career, a lot of mirror-imaging that seems crafted and pre-determined; except it can't be, save in the sense that the laws of evolution or the movements of the planets are schematic, and beyond the control of con-sciousness or human intervention. The famous man, not as famous as he'd like to have been, or famous for the wrong reasons; a star, yet he couldn't afford the opulence and the trappings of stardom; he was reclusive, yet note how he put himself about, dining in shops; he was thrifty, yet liked to be amidst bric-à-brac and clutter and dresses. Hawtrey created a cheerful, sunny persona, yet he was as sweet as strychnine; he was part of the history of British popular culture, yet he wanted to eradicate himself; he didn't want to belong to history, or to anyone, threatening legal action or rabbit punches if his very existence was alleged. In his work there is enjoyment, a winningness; in his life, furtiveness, pride, cynicism, boredom and hatred, a strain of discord forever creaking and snapping beneath the surface. In the photo-graphs of him creeping about Deal ('I particularly remember he was very angry to see the photographer Basil Kidd outside his house,' says Joy Leonard), his face has fallen into a tragic aspect; his laughter, to those who heard it in the street, had become hollow and manic; and his conversation, Joan Sims said to me, was a psychotic babble: 'He'd phone me up and be on the line for hours – this meaningless gurgling and sighing. This very lonely sad little man . . . '

Lonely. I think that has to be the summation of him in the end. On his tongue the taste was sour of all he ever did. My abiding image is a glimpse of him at the wedding of Ernest Maxin to Leigh Madison. 'He arrived in full array,' says Norman Hudis, 'a long dark overcoat and an Anthony Eden hat – entirely suitable for a Jewish ceremony but distinctly odd on him. As the couple left the synagogue, I happened to glance past them – to Charlie, wide-eyed under the brim of that absurd hat, looking at the newly weds unblinkingly, with something between envy and sorrow. I shall never forget that look. Pagliacci was a boisterous self-confident figure by comparison.'

We can blame the booze for the hallucinations and delirium. We may also claim that alcohol released the bottled goblin that was already dwelling within him. It can be said with certainty, however, that the destructive addiction which did duly finish him off was to nicotine. On 24 October 1988, Hawtrey tried to enter the Royal Hotel, on the seafront near the pier, around the corner from Middle Street. He was in a drunken stupor and collapsed in the doorway. He shattered his femur and was rushed in an ambulance to the Buckland Hospital, Dover. His broken upper leg was less of a problem than the state of his withered, wasted arteries. Decades of smoking had caused a condition called peripheral vascular disease. Gangrene was setting in. The doctor who informed him that he must lose both of his legs by amputation or die happened to be the elder sister of Alan James Watson, the little boy he'd told to 'Piss off!' Hawtrey refused the drastic operation. Not even the notion that he'd now have a pego that literally dragged the floor could persuade the size queen who'd appeared in *What a Whopper!* to go through with it. Nor the blandishment that there'd be a saving on the cost of wood for a short coffin. He asked if his wrecked blood vessels could be replaced with, say, pig's veins, was told no and shunted into a small side ward. Even on his deathbed he refused to let the medical staff have his autograph. As soon as Watson heard that Hawtrey was in his sister's care, he asked her to get his signature, to no avail. 'Piss off!' he yelled, threw a vase at her, and then the trumpet sounded and he died.

Hawtrey had been legless often enough in his life not to want to go the whole hog. In any event, he was beyond arterial reconstructive surgery, endarterectomy (the removal of the fatty deposits from blood-vessel linings) or angioplasty (a widening of narrowed veins). Barbara Windsor is right to point out how courageously he died, how stoical he was. As she told me, 'He may have been a bit of an oddball, Charlie, but he was a brave one. When he was dying and his doctors told him they would have to amputate his legs, he lit a fag and said, "No – I want to die with my boots on!" And that's what he did.'

Nine people attended his obsequies, held at Mortlake Crematorium on Hallowe'en. The venue had been changed twice, to put off the press, because as Philip Warner, the curate, said, 'Charles was in public life but didn't want to become public property.' Gerald Thomas remarked, 'If he'd really had his wish, he'd have been the only person at the funeral.' Once you've subtracted the vicar, organist, undertakers and cemetery staff from the congregation, clearly the wish had come true. Of Hawtrey's former showbusiness colleagues, only Barbara Windsor and Frankie Howerd bothered to send cards and flowers. Kenneth Williams had committed suicide six months earlier, on 15 April. Hawtrey, who was intestate, left £163,165 (£164,929 gross). What became of that? Where are his ashes scattered? Were there no family attachments?* It's not inappropriate that I don't know. He yearned to vanish, to vaporize, so let's let him do so; in a swirl of smoke, like a genie in a pantomime, or like his mortal remains in the Mortlake incinerator, off he goes: the man who was Big Heap, Tonka, Sir Roger de Lodgerley, and Private Widdle.

> *Not a flower, not a flower sweet,*
> *On my black coffin let there be strown;*
> *Not a friend, not a friend greet*
> *My poor corpse where my bones shall be thrown . . .*

* On his deathbed Hawtrey raved confusedly that he wanted to find his vanished eighty-two-year-old brother, who'd run away to Australia decades before. Could such a man possibly have existed – or exist still? What long-tangled *Prisoner of Zenda*, *I due Foscari*, *Twelfth Night* and *Prince and the Pauper* psychodramas are suggested here? An Austral Hawtrey (or Hartree) would be ninety-five at the present time – not impossible. I'm picturing an epicene boy in the bush who grew up to become perhaps Barry Humphries' grandfather – for is there not already an imaginative link between Hawtrey's transvestism and Dame Edna's pantyhose? Humphries himself also possesses ('bought on some absurd caprice') a pair of fine cambric bloomers trimmed with lace and blue ribbon that had once belonged to Heather Firbank, sister of the novelist Ronald Firbank – another Hawtrey-esque personage, God knows.

Epilogue

On 9 September 1987, Kenneth Williams wrote to his friend Jeffrey Kemp, a retired teacher who lived in France, about a visit he'd made to see Hawtrey in Kent.

[. . .] You were not supposed to laugh about Charlie Hawtrey being hauled out of the fire, with the boyfriend languishing in the bed and the fags uncollected. It is supposed to have a tragic ring, like the 'Wreck of the Deutschland' or something.* People are always writing asking me how they can get in touch with him. It is all otiose 'cos he never answers letters. When he first retired to Deal I went down there with some friends to visit. Banged and banged at the door to no avail. Eventually a window on the opposite side screeched open and a woman with the hair in curlers shouted rudely 'You after Charlie?' 'Mister Hawtrey,' I returned haughtily. 'We were seeking Mister Hawtrey!' 'Try the Saracen's Head,' she bawled and shut the window. Well we must have visited half the pubs in the neighbourhood, but eventually CH was found. Rather the worse for wear. Insisted on taking us to tea with these 'Wonderful friends of mine that have a little café where they make EVERYTHING with their own HOME stone ground flour.' After eating one of their cakes, I think I got the stone. Felt like a foundation stone. Just sank into the stomach relentlessly. Took a lot of bicarb & farting to shift it. O never again. As we walked along the front, fishermen eyed us warily. Charlie was in orange trousers, blue shirt and silk scarf at the neck. He was carrying his umbrella as a parasol. The day was quite fine. The rest of us were trying to look anonymous. 'Hallo

* Gerard Manley Hopkins' poem (1875), about drowned nuns, is far from rib-tickling. Anthony Burgess contemplated making a Hollywood film-script out of it. (See *The Clockwork Testament*, 1974.)

lads!' he kept calling out to men painting their boats. 'They all adore me here,' he told us, 'brings a bit of glamour into their dull lives.' They smiled back uneasily, and certainly some returned his salutations, but I didn't get the impression of universal adoration. The house was awful. Everywhere you went there were these huge brass beds. 'They'll come back into fashion one day & I'll make a fortune!' he declared as he rubbed them affectionately. Then he recited an endless saga about some boys from the Royal Marines School of Music carousing with him round the local hostelries & all piling back to his place to stay the night: 'And just LOOK at what they gave me to show their appreciation!' he cried, thrusting a huge portfolio in front of us. Somebody asked nervously 'What is it?' and with extraordinary triumph CH announced 'The original score of THE BOHEMIAN GIRL.' He kept on about this being an original and repeating that it had 'the Vienna stamp on it' but the whole thing smacked of fraudulence. What on earth has Balfe to do with Vienna, one asks oneself.*

yours,

Kenneth

---

* What indeed. Michael William Balfe was born in Dublin in 1808, studied abroad under Rossini, and after the success of *The Bohemian Girl*, in 1843, was appointed conductor of the London Italian Opera Company. He died in 1870. Perhaps Hawtrey was thinking of Rudolf Friml and *The Maid of the Mountains*? Or had Williams misheard and it had 'the Venetian stamp on it', which could have meant the score of *Grab Me a Gondola*, a musical that had starred Denis Quilley? *The Bohemian Girl* premièred at Drury Lane and was revived by Sadler's Wells in 1932 and by Sir Thomas Beecham at Covent Garden in 1951. The farrago deals with gypsies and noblemen and unfolds in Poland and – yes – Austria. This, Wallace's *Maritana* and Benedict's *The Lily of Killarney* were collectively known as 'The English Ring', according to my Kobbé.

Appendix

217 Cromwell Road,
Hounslow. Middlesex.

HOU 0636   1–12–54

Mike Meehan, Esq.,
B.B.C.
Aeolian Hall,
135, New Bond Street,
London. W.1.

Dear Mr. Mike Meehan,
                    Since the end of the series 'Ray's a Laugh', I
seem to be neglected by the Variety Department, and I should be very
grateful indeed if you would try and find something for me. My work
outside the Corporation might be of some interest to you, and I enclose
a résumé of my past work. This however, does not include Cabaret
engagements. By the way, many moons ago I was given an audition by
the Variety Deparment, and judging by the letter following, passed it,
but nothing has happened yet.
Looking forward to seeing you again.*
                    With kindest regards,
                    Yours sincerely,

                    Charles Hawtrey

---

* Meehan gave Hawtrey the bum's rush by return: 'I am sorry to hear Variety
producers have not been in touch with you for some time. They, of course,
know your work very well and I will remind them that you are still in the land
of the very active living.'

The Man who was Private Widdle

Here follows Hawtrey's painstakingly typed résumé that was enclosed with his letter of 1 December 1954 to Mike Meehan. Any errors, omissions or aggrandisements are wholly his own.

Films *

1931 *Marry Me*, Gainsborough
1932 *The Melody Maker*, Warner Bros.
1933 *Case Hardened*, Warner Bros.
     Devil to Pay, Warner Bros.
     High Finance, Warner Bros.
     Smithy, Warner Bros.
     Good as New, Warner Bros.
     Office Wives, Warner Bros.

---

* As lengthy as this list is, the National Film and Television Archive reckons that Hawtrey was also in *Kiddies on Parade* (1935), *Melody and Romance* (1937), where he recites Shakespeare at an audition, and *Hammer the Toff* (1952). Post-1954 there were the *Carry On*s, of course, which began tickling us to bits in 1958, plus *Simon and Laura* (1955), where he was a railway porter; *Time Slip* (1955) – an office boy; *Who Done It?* (1956) – disc jockey; *The March Hare* (1956) – Fisher; *The Army Game* (1957) – cast member; *I Only Arsked!* (1958) – the professor; *Please Turn Over* (1959) – jeweller; *Inn for Trouble* (1959) – Silas; *Our House* (1960) – Simon Willow; *Dentist on the Job* (1961) – chemist; *What a Whopper!* (1961) – Arnold; *The Terrornauts* (1967) – Yellowlees; *Zeta One* (1969) – Swyne; *Stop Exchange* (1970) – cast member; *The Princess and the Pea* (1979) – cast member; *Supergran and the State Visit* (1987) – Clarence, Duke of Claridge. The final two (children's television shows) are intriguing as it had been my belief that Hawtrey was one of the Undead by this period. Do write to me if you have any background information.

STOP PRESS. Craig Brown claims to have seen *Supergran*, and that Supergran was Molly Weir, a diminutive Scottish actress not to be confused with Gudrun Ure or Barbara Mullen. Molly may best be remembered as the scold in outsize yellow Marigolds leaning over a tub and assuring us that 'Flash cleans baths without scratching' – which begs the question, what previously did they use to scour their *en suite* facilities in north Britain pre-Molly? Sandpaper? Igneous grit?

Appendix

1934 *Murder at Monte Carlo*, Warner Bros.
Little Stranger, Warner Bros.
Trouble in Store, Warner Bros.
Mayfair Girl, Warner Bros.
Gay Lord Strathpeffer, Warner Bros.
Hyde Park, Warner Bros.
Man With a Million, Warner Bros.

1935 *Water Nymph*, Warner Bros.
Windfall, Walton-on-Thames
Money by Wire, Warner Bros.
The Brown Wallet, Warner Bros.
Well Done Henry, Butchers

1936 *Good Morning Boys*, Gainsborough
East of Ludgate Hill, Fox British

1937 *Sabotage*, Gaumont British

1938 *Where's That Fire*, Gainsborough
Boys Will be Boys, Warner Bros. [Gainsborough]

1939 *Jailbirds*, Butchers

1940 *Ghost of St. Michael's*, Ealing

1941 *Goose Steps Out*, Warner Bros. [Ealing]

1942 *Much Too Shy*, Elstree
Let the People Sing, British National

1943 *Bell Bottomed George*, Gainsborough

1944 *Ten Year Plan*, G.B.I.
Canterbury Tale, Archers

1946 *Meet Me at Dawn*, Excelsior

1947 *End of the River*, Independent

1948 *Shirley Yorke*, Nettlefold
Passport to Pimlico, Ealing

1949 *Dark Secret*, Nettlefold
Room to Let, Exclusive

1950 *Smart Alec*, Vandyke
Galloping Major, Sirius

1951 *Brandy for the Parson*, Group 3
You're Only Young Twice, Warner Bros. [Group 3]

1953 *Five Days*, Exclusive

1954 *To Dorothy a Son*, Welbeck
As Long as They're Happy, Pinewood

The Man who was Private Widdle

Theatre*

1925 *The Windmill Man*, Tour
1927 *Bluebell in Fairyland*, Scala
1928 *Where the Rainbow Ends*, Holborn Empire
1929 *Quality Street*, Haymarket
House that Jack Built, Tour
Babes in the Wood, Exeter
1930 *Love's Labour's Lost*, Haymarket
Street Scene, Globe
1931 *Cavalcade*, Drury Lane
Peter Pan, Palladium
Evergreen, Adelphi
1934 *The Maitlands*, Leeds
1936 *Your Numbers Up*, Gate
Peter Pan, Palladium
1937 *Bats in the Belfry*, Ambassadors
Members Only, Gate
1938 *Strange Family*, Q Theatre
Chain Male, Richmond
Happy Returns, Adelphi
1939 *Printers Devil*, Embassy
Taming of the Shrew, The Old Vic
Counterfeit!, Duke of York's
1940 *Without the Prince*, Richmond
New Faces, Comedy & Apollo
1941 *Ambassadors' Revue*, Ambassadors
1942 *Scoop!*, Vaudeville
1943 *Old Chelsea*, Princes
Housemaster, Q Theatre
Claudius the Bee, Q Theatre
1944 *Merrie England*, Winter Garden
1945 *Variety with Will Hay*, Victoria Palace
1947 *Vice Versa*, Q Theatre
1950 *Frou Frou*, New Lindsay

* Thereafter there was the tour of Sondheim/Shevelove/Gelbart's *A Funny Thing Happened on the Way to the Forum* (what's its perennial appeal for old comics?), end-of-the-pier shows and pantomimes in the back of beyond, many produced by Aubrey Phillips.

Appendix

1951 *Husbands Dont Count*, New Lindsay
1952 *Husbands Dont Count*, Winter Garden
1953 *Bless You*, Q Theatre

Film Direction*

What Do We Do Now?
with Moon & Brown, Harry Parry Band, Ronald Frankau, Edmundo
Ros Band, Barrie Lupino, Percival Mackey Band (Grand National)

* Prints no longer seem to exist of the two films Hawtrey directed. *What Do We Do Now?* was made in 1945 and had a running-time of seventy-five minutes. George Moon and Burton Brown played Lesley and Wesley, comedians awaiting their turn at the Skewball Hippodrome. They become amateur detectives to find a stolen diamond brooch. The story is interspersed with music-hall acts, including Seffani and his Thirty Silver Songsters. Listed in the billing is Jill Summers, who'd play the gravel-voiced basso profundo Phyllis Pearce in *Coronation Street*. The screenplay was by George A. Cooper. Hawtrey was his own Director of Photography. Reviews and full credits may be found in *Kinematograph Weekly* (17 January 1946), *Today's Cinema* (11 July 1946) and the *Monthly Film Bulletin*, Volume 13, page 3.

The correct title of his other effort is *Dumb Dora Discovers Tobacco*. It was released in 1946 at a length of forty-two minutes. Dumb Dora is a bimbo journalist, attempting to research an article on the origins of smoking and (let's speculate) what it is like to cough up tar. Henry Kendall had appeared with Hawtrey in revue; Claud Allister is the monocled silly-ass in *Bulldog Drummond*; God knows who Pamela Stirling is or was. Also in the cast – Flora Robson, star of *Fire Over England* and much else besides. The *Monthly Film Bulletin* mentioned the film in Volume 13 (January 1946) and Volume 14 (September 1947); *Today's Cinema* refers to it in the issues of 15 January 1946 and 21 August 1947. *Kinematograph Weekly* reviewed it on 17 January 1946 and 21 August 1947. For its re-release, in 1947, ten minutes were lopped off and it was retitled *Fag End*.

Working on this book, I got so absorbed in Hawtrey I even laughed about him in my sleep and I dreamt an entire film for him, called *Milly and the Milk* – a *Carry On* about a dairy distribution centre. Sid James, who drove an Aston Martin sprayed Jewish Racing Gold, wore sunglasses and organized the milk-float rota. Barbara Windsor was a milkmaid – hence lots of jokes about udders, milk jugs and blue tits pecking her silver top. Hawtrey was the depot's time and motion man, hovering and whirling and at his most Gielgudian: the snooty posture, the airs he gives himself, his astringency and refinement in the midst of boob and erection gags. This is such a plausible scenario, maybe it does exist.

The Man who was Private Widdle

Dumb Dora
with Henry Kendall, Claud Allister, Pamela Stirling (Grand National)

Stage Production*

Czechmate with Joan Greenwood
By Candlelight with Magda Kum
Temporary Ladies with Peggy Cummins
Trial of Mary Dugan with Alice Gachet
Oflag 3 with Julian Dallas
Peg of My Heart with Eileen Thorndike
Trouble in the House with Gus McNaughton
Chinese Bungalow with Joan Greenwood
Other People's Houses with Helen Goss
Mother of Men with Barbara Mullen
The Blue Lamp with Fred Kitchen

* As a stage director, Hawtrey (who did not furnish this list with any dates) worked at the Q Theatre, Kew Bridge, Brentford (approximate seating capacity, 497). I have obtained a programme for *Temporary Ladies* by Eileen Ellett, which ran for a week from 21–27 May 1945. 'The action of the play takes place in the lobby and ante-room of an ATS officers' mess in southern England . . . Attention is drawn to air raid warnings during Act II which are part of the play.' I also possess a playbill for *Oflag 3* ('The scene is a room in an Officers' Prison Camp in Germany . . . Properties kindly loaned by the British Red Cross and St. John and Canadian Red Cross'), which ran from 26 June to 1 July 1945. The authors were Flight Lieutenant Douglas Bader, Squadron Leader Armitage and Flight Lieutenant Hugh Falkus. That these heroes entrusted Hawtrey of all people with their *gesamtkunstwerk* showed real bravery indeed.

Mother of Men by Ada G. Abbott was produced in the last week of July 1946 and transferred to the Comedy Theatre, Panton Street, in September. The star, Barbara Mullen, was later Dr Finlay's housekeeper, Janet. ('Och, Dr Finlay, I think I've got heartburn.' 'Ney, Janet lass, take your tit out o' the porridge.') Leonard Mosley wrote: 'There is the illegitimate child, and the girl who dives into the sea to drown her shame about it. There is the son who steals from his Mam to buy trinkets for the lightsome lady from London. There is even an irate father . . . [The author] apparently forgot to say whether she meant it to be taken very seriously, and the producer has merely called it "a simple story". It is very simple [. . .] and most of the situations in this play should be taken with a hearty laugh rather than a nervous giggle.' (*Daily Express*, 12 September 1946.)

Appendix

Happy Birthday with Mary Clare
Happiest Days of Your Life with Viola Lyel
Uncle Harry with Wally Patch
Murder in Mayfair with Tonie Edgar Bruce
How Are They at Home with Anthony Nicolls
The Perfect Woman with Violet Loxley
Guest in the House with Rene Ray
Young Man's Fancy with Violet Farebrother
You Can't Take It with You with Bessie Love

SELECT BIBLIOGRAPHY

- 'Lasting tribute to a man who brought laughter', *East Kent Mercury* (19 November 1998).
- National Theatre Programme for *Cleo, Camping, Emmanuelle and Dick* by Terry Johnson, Lyttelton Theatre (September 1998).

Booth, Mark, *Camp* (London, 1983).

Box, Betty, *Lifting the Lid: The Autobiography of Film Producer Betty Box, OBE* (London, 2000).

Briggs, Sue, 'Carry On with fond memories as Hawtrey's life is honoured,' *East Kent Mercury* (12 November 1998).

Bright, Morris and Ross, Robert, *Carry On Uncensored* (London, 1999).

- *The Lost Carry Ons* (London, 2000).
- *Mr Carry On: The Life and Work of Peter Rogers* (London, 2000).

Cashin, Fergus, 'Carry On, what's his name!' *Sun* (16 August 1972).

Coward, Noël, *Autobiography* (London, 1986).

Eastaugh, Kenneth, *The Carry On Book* (London, 1978).

Gielgud, John, *Backward Glances* (London, 1989).

Hanson, Bruce K., *The Peter Pan Chronicles* (New York, 1993).

Hibbin, Sally and Nina, *What a Carry On: The Official Story of the Carry On Film Series* (London, 1988).

Massingberd, Hugh (ed.), *The Daily Telegraph Third Book of Obituaries: Entertainers* (London, 1997).

Naish, John, 'Cor, what a lovely pair of fireplaces', *The Times* (23 September 2000).

Rigelsford, Adrian, *Carry on Laughing: A Celebration* (London, 1996).

Ross, Robert, *The Carry On Companion* (London, 1996).

Salter, Elizabeth, *Helpmann: The Authorized Biography of Sir Robert Helpmann, CBE* (Brighton, 1978).

Sims, Joan, *High Spirits* (London, 2000).

Wapshott, Tim, 'Carry On Star Saved in Blaze', *Sun* (6 August 1984).

The Man who was Private Widdle

Watkins, Alan *et al.*, 'Sad Star Who Has to Carry On Boozing', *Sun* (29 September 1988).

Williams, Kenneth, *Diaries* ed. Russell Davies (London, 1993).

– *Just Williams: An Autobiography* (London, 1985).

– *Letters* ed. Russell Davies (London, 1994).

Windsor, Barbara, *All of Me: My Extraordinary Life* (London, 2000).

INDEX

Page references followed by 'n' are to footnotes, and those in italics are to illustrations.

Agate, James 7
Alice in Wonderland 23, 77
Arlen, Albert 36
Arlen, Harold 26
Auric, Georges 62

Baddeley, Hermione 64
Balcon, Michael 62
Balfe, Michael William 98n
Balzac, Honoré de 28
Barrie, Amanda 35
Barrie, J.M. 7, 10
Bats in the Belfry 18
Baxter, Stanley 29
British Broadcasting Corporation
  (BBC) 23–5, 31, 61–2, 65–9
Beardsley, Aubrey 33
Beddgelert 6n
Benny, Jack 16
Benson, E. F. 22
Bentley, John 21, 29
Bergman, Ingmar 28
Best, George 68, 77
Betjeman, John 5n
The Bohemian Girl 98
Bourner, Colin 87–8
Box, Betty 75
Bresslaw, Bernard 4, 6, 16n, 35,
  83–4
Brown, Pamela 22n
Browning, Robert 28n
Bullock, Barry 85
Burgess, Anthony 22n, 97n
Burton, Josephine 69
Butcher, Cyril 36

Butterworth, Peter 4, 32, 35
Byng, Dougie 29

Camber Sands 4, 6n
Campbell, Judy 26–7
A Canterbury Tale 28
Carney, Terry 72
Carry On films 3–7, 11, 14, 17–18,
  28, 30, 35–6, 43n, 65, 73, 76
  ... *Abroad* 14–15, 33, 44, 74n,
    79–80
  ... *Again Doctor* 13, 16, 30–1, 56
  ... *Cabby* 43
  ... *Camping* 4, 11, 13–14, 30,
    42–3
  ... *Christmas* 25, 74
  ... *Cleo* 21, 30, 34–5, 48
  ... *Constable* 29, 37, 48
  ... *Columbus* 5
  ... *at your Convenience* 4, 6, 13,
    33, 36n, 39, 79
  ... *Cowboy* 4, 6, 78
  ... *Cruising* 18, 73
  ... *Doctor* 4, 6, 13, 30, 33, 79, 84
  ... *Henry* 81
  ... *Jack* 5
  ... *Loving* 34–5
  ... *Matron* 4, 13
  ... *Nurse* 13
  ... *Regardless* 16
  ... *Screaming* 43–4
  ... *Sergeant* 18
  ... *Spying* 7, 33, 79
  ... *Teacher* 34, 43
  ... *Up the Jungle* 5, 30, 77, 84, 86

... *Up the Khyber* 4, 6n, 21, 55, 88
Castle, Roy 88
Chaplin, Charlie 24, 79
Chesterton, G. K. 22
Chitty Chitty Bang Bang 23, 70
Clark, Joan 66n
Clary, Julian 5
Cleese, John 42
Cleo, Camping, Emmanuelle and Dick 38
Cochran, Charles B. 25, 27
Cocteau, Jean 33, 62
Coe, Jonathan 36n, 63n
Congreve, William 36
Connor, Kenneth 35–6
Conrad, Joseph 39
Conti, Italia 10, 12–13
Cook, Peter 83
Cooper, Tommy 16
Cor Blimey! 38n
Counterfeit! 36–7, 45
Coward, Noël 7–20 *passim* 27
Crisp, Quentin 15–16
Crompton, Richmal 25
Crow, Alice 9; *see also* Hawtrey, Charles: mother
Curzon, George 7

Daily Express 38
Daily Telegraph 37
Dale, Jim 30, 32
Davies, Robertson 22n
Desmonde, Jerry 42n
Dick Whittington 19, 83
Dillon, Carmen 18
Don't Lose Your Head 19, 30–1, 42, 75
du Maurier, Gerald 17n
Dudley, William 38
'Dunne, Alice' 87

Ellis, Walter 64
Emery, Dick 29
Esmond, Jill 19
Evans, Edith 13n

Fellini, Federico 28
Firbank, Heather 93n
Follow That Camel 4, 6n, 32
Forbes-Robertson, Jean 7
A Funny Thing Happened on the Way to the Forum 23
Furse, Roger 22

Garbo, Greta 83
German, Sir Edward 64
Gershwin, Ira 26
The Ghost of St Michael's 42–3
Gielgud, John 8, 11–12
Glyn-Jones, John 72
Good Morning Boys 43
The Goose Steps Out 40, 42–3
Guinness, Alec 9, 19
Guthrie, Tyrone 22–3

Happy Returns 25–6
Hartree, William John 9
Hassall, Imogen 73
Hawk, Jeremy 21
Hawkins, Jack 18
Hawtrey, Charles
  acting style 11–16, 21, 32–3, 42–4, 68
  and autographs 15, 81–2, 91
  birth 8–9
  broadcasting work 23–5, 61–2, 65–9
  in cabaret 66
  death 83, 91–2
  depression and sense of failure 76–83 *passim* 86, 89
  drinking 77–82, 86, 91
  early stage performances 7, 10, 25
  failure to find work 55–7, 61, 66–9
  family 93n
  father 9
  first gramophone recording 3
  grievances over billing 71–5, 77
  homosexuality 14, 68, 69n, 78, 98
  house in Deal 84–5, 88–9
  last appearances in pantomime 83
  limitations of career 19, 23–5, 28, 65, 84

Index

mother 9, 37–8, 70, 76, 87–9
  as a musical artiste 65–6
  physical appearance 18, 20, 22, 33, 35, 40–1
  playing women 31–2, 36–9
  private and social life 12–13, 20, 70, 80
  pseudonym ('Alice Dunne') 87
  reclusiveness 15, 81–2, 86–90
  in revue 25–9, 65
  sex life 81–2
  smoking 91
  use of taxis 86, 88–9
  wearing of costume 33–4
Hawtrey, Sir Charles 8–12 passim 15, 17
Hay, Will 40–3, 62, 64–5
Hayes, Patricia 25, 72–3
Hazlitt, William 34
Helpmann, Robert 18, 21–3, 79
Hitchcock, Alfred 39
Holloway, Stanley 63–4
Hopkins, Gerald Manley 97n
Houston, Renee 79
Howerd, Frankie 33, 68, 83–4, 92
Hudis, Norman 15, 80, 90–1
Humphries, Barry 29, 93n
Huntley, Raymond 63
Husbands Don't Count 62

'I Don't Want to Play in Your Yard' 3
Italia Conti drama school 10–13, 18
Izzard, Eddie 68

Jacques, Hattie 28, 35, 70, 74, 81
James, Sid 4, 28, 30, 34–5, 38, 74n, 86
Jeans, Ursula 22
Joffre, Joseph Jacques Césaire 9
Johnson, Bryan 71
Johnson, Terry 38n
Jones, D. Emrys 6n
Just William 25

Kelly, Matthew 69
Kemp, Jeffrey 97

Kendall, Henry 28
Kidd, Basil 90
Kipling, Rudyard 4n

La Rue, Danny 29, 43n
Lamb, Charles 36
Lanchester, Elsa 7–8
Larkin, Philip 76, 88–9
Laughton, Charles 7
Laurel, Stan 24
Lautrec, Toulouse 35–6
Laye, Dilys 14, 79
Leigh, Vivien 18–19, 71, 78
Leon, Valerie 31
Leonard, Joy 20, 82, 90
Lillie, Beatrice 26, 78
Livesey, Roger 22n
Lom, Herbert 42n
Love's Labours Lost 25n
Loving 73

McGrath, Joe 80
Madison, Leigh 90
Manderson, David 69–70
Marriott, Moore 40
Marsden, Betty 11
Maugham, Somerset 8
Maxin, Ernest 80, 90
Maxwell, Charles 66n
Mayall, Rik 5
Menges, Herbert 22
Merrie England 64–5
Moffatt, Graham 40
Moore, Dudley 83
Morecambe, Eric 16
Murray, Bertram and Mrs 12

Naish, John 85n
National Theatre 38
The New Ambassadors' Review 27, 29
New Faces 21, 26–7, 29, 46
Newington, Peter 77
Newley, Patrick 82–3
Newman, Pat 66
Norman and Henry Bones 25, 72–3
Norton, Graham 68–9

Novello, Ivor 68

O'Callaghan, Richard 73
The *Observer* 37
Old Chelsea 64–5
Olivier, Laurence 16–19, 71
Orton, Joe 5n
Orwell, George 6n
Our House 80

Parker, Al 62, 69
Passport to Pimlico 62–3
Patricia Cornish Pantomime Babes 19
Percheron, Betty 64–5
Percival, Lance 73
Perelman, S. J. 21
Peter Pan 7–10
Pheloung, Barrington 38
Phillips, Leslie 12
Piffard, Freddie 66n
Pinewood Studios 12, 70
Piper, Jacki 73
Plath, Sylvia 18
Please Turn Over 62
Poets' Corner 12
Portman, Eric 37
Pound, Ezra 5n
Present Laughter 13
Price, Dennis 28
Private Lives 13, 18

Quilley, Denis 38, 99

Radford, Basil 63
Radio Who's Who 24
Rank Organization 74
Redgrave, Michael 16
Richards, Cyril 27
Riggs, Geoffrey E. O. 66
Robinson Clarke, Katharine Elsie 8n
Rockingham Club 82
Rogers, Peter 13, 18n, 31–2, 34, 42, 62, 74–80
Romberg, Sigmund 68
Ross, Robert 74n
Rothwell, Talbot 13, 83–4, 85n

Rowlands, Patsy 35
Royal Marines School of Music 81, 98
Rutherford, Margaret 63
Rutherford, Norman 61
Rylance, Mark 5n

Sabotage 39
Sargent, Malcolm 34
Sayle, Alexei 5
Scales, Prunella 42n
Scoop! 27–9, 47
Scott, Terry 21, 28, 74n
Scott-Johnson, A. 66n
Sellers, Peter 42n
Sendak, Maurice 5n
Sherrin, Ned 83–4
Silvers, Phil 32
Sims, Joan 4, 14, 17, 37–8, 42, 90
Smith, Gordon 62
So Graham Norton 68–9n
Spiro, Samantha 38n
The Stage 37
Stewart, Hugh 24
Stop It Nurse! 19
Sykes, Eric 74

Tauber, Richard 64, 78
Thames Television 73–4
Theatre Royal, Exeter 10–11
Thesiger, Ernest 22, 27, 29
Thomas, Gerald 13, 32, 74–7, 92
The Times 27–8, 37, 65
To Dorothy a Son 62
Topolski, Feliks 29
'Tree, Charlotte' 37, 45
Trevelyan, John 31
Twelfth Night 19, 21, 23n
Tynan, Kenneth 16

Up Pompeii 83–4
Updike, John 89

Van Ost, Valerie 42

Walters, Hugh 38n
Ward, Bill 62

Index

Warner, Philip 92
Warren, Betty 64
Washbourne, Mona 62n
Watson, Alan James 82, 91
Wayne, Naunton 63
Welles, Orson 5n
Welty, Eudora 21
What a Carry On 8
Where the Rainbow Ends 10–11, 18
Whitfield, June 74, 80
Wilde, Oscar 16, 43n, 69
Wilder, Billy 36n

Williams, Kenneth 4, 7, 11–12,
    17, 18n, 19–21, 28–30, 32,
    35, 38n, 43n, 64, 74, 75–9,
    84, 88–9, 92, 97
Williams, Tennessee 83
Windsor, Barbara 4, 28, 68, 74,
    77–8, 92
Winton, Dale 68–9
Wisdom, Norman 42

Young, Arthur 21